MILLIGAN'S FIGHT AGAINST LINCOLN

MILLIGAN'S FIGHT AGAINST LINCOLN

Darwin Kelley

With a Foreword by L. E. Carlson

An Exposition-University Book
EXPOSITION PRESS   NEW YORK

EXPOSITION PRESS, INC.

50 Jericho Turnpike, Jericho, New York 11753

FIRST EDITION

© 1973 by Darwin Kelley. *All rights reserved including the right of reproduction in whole or in part in any form except for short quotations in critical essays and reviews.* Manufactured in the United States of America.

LIBRARY OF CONGRESS CATALOG CARD NUMBER: 72-94854

SBN 0-682-47651-X

Contents

FOREWORD by L. E. Carlson — vii

PREFACE — xi

I	Introduction	3
II	Decisions for Square Away	6
III	Locale of Milligan	15
IV	Historical Background	20
V	Change Accepted by Lincoln, 1861-1862	32
VI	Change Resisted by Milligan, 1861-1862	45
VII	Triumph of Lincoln, 1863-1864	58
VIII	Milligan Antagonizing Precedents, 1863-1864	72
IX	Civil Rights Victory	95

APPENDIX: Statement by Milligan at the Trial of Alexander J. Douglas — 112

INDEX — 117

Foreword

This book brings into sharp focus the intensity of feeling in Huntington County during the Civil War period.

All the actors in that tragic drama of over a century ago have long since passed from the stage of activity, but their roles and the scenes of conflict remain in poignant memory. These are brought back alive by the author, Dr. Darwin Kelley of Huntington, Indiana.

The central character portrayed in the book is Lambdin P. Milligan, a Huntington lawyer then in his late forties, a man of outstanding legal ability. Tall, broad-shouldered and fair-haired, he was an irreconcilable opponent of the Civil War. His fiery speeches against the war and the Lincoln Administration caused great concern among many of his neighbors and friends, and aroused the fierce hostility of his enemies, earning him the epithet of "traitor."

Milligan was a student of constitutional law and held unshakable views with respect to certain of its provisions. His opinion was that under the United States Constitution the several states of the Union retained a sphere of sovereignty. His position was that since the original thirteen colonies as sovereign states had voluntarily united together in a union of sovereign states they could *ipso facto* as sovereign states withdraw or secede from this union, since the Federal Constitution which they adopted and approved contained no explicit provision to the contrary.

As the desperate war years wore on, death and destruction mounted, affecting in some way great or small a large part of the population of Huntington County.

A succession of military defeats suffered by the North caused great anxiety, uncertainty as to the outcome, and frustration.

In this atmosphere of growing pressure and deep concern, the military authorities at Indianapolis finally determined to arrest Milligan.

Accordingly, a short train on the Wabash Railroad, which adjoined Milligan's house and yard just west of Huntington, backed up to his home with a squadron of troops on board. They seized Milligan and took him to Indianapolis where he was tried before a military tribunal, charged with treason, found guilty, and sentenced to be hanged as a traitor.

In the subsequent proceedings involving the writ of habeas corpus the case was appealed to the United States Supreme Court. While Milligan was known as a radical Democrat he was represented by such eminent counsel as James A. Garfield, a Republican who later became president of the United States.

President Lincoln had indicated his disapproval of these and other similar proceedings which involved other outspoken critics of the war. He would have stayed the sentence against Milligan except for his assassination on April 14, 1865. Andrew Johnson, who succeeded Lincoln as president, refused to interfere with the sentence of death, but Edwin M. Stanton, secretary of war in the Lincoln and Johnson administrations and a former classmate of Milligan, was instrumental in reducing the sentence to life imprisonment.

The Supreme Court in a landmark decision in constitutional law held that no person not in the military service could be tried by military court-martial while the civil courts were open, and accordingly Milligan was freed.

After his release from prison as a result of the court decision, Milligan returned to Huntington, where he practiced law as a leading member of the bar until his death during the last days of the last century.

This book is a scholarly treatise. It is well documented and gives the reader the distinct feeling that he is actually living among the people of that time and place. It correctly reflects the views of Milligan on the war, states' rights, civil rights, and the other great questions of the day about which he expressed himself. While many did not then and do not now agree with Milligan, they all respect his courage and ability to champion a generally unpopular posi-

Foreword

tion without regard to his own personal safety or consequences.

This book is a great contribution to the history of Huntington County and through Milligan its relationship with the national government during a trying period of its history.

L. E. CARLSON

Preface

Lambdin P. Milligan was "a heroic character in many respects," with "the courage of his convictions,"[1] who fought against President Abraham Lincoln.[2] Milligan was so completely defeated by Indiana Republicans and War Democrats on the question of states' rights that Lincoln was more helped than harmed. He paid no attention to Milligan. This would have ended the matter had it not been for Milligan's tenacity and strength in law for civil rights.

Milligan's final statement to the Huntington County Bar, presented before lawyers who knew him well, shows why Republicans as well as Democrats came to esteem the vital principle of the lesser man in the fight: "Respect the law, respect the court as one of its institutions, and above all . . . respect yourselves, remembering that a trickster cannot be a lawyer."[3] As for himself, Milligan said: "If I have merited any distinction in my practice or life, it is in antagonizing precedents not founded on legal reasons."[4]

This little book is the product of a labor of love for many years. My purpose is to share the story of a seminal newspaper battle and Milligan's dedication to law. With many others I regret the paucity of his remains.

I wish to thank Howard Houghton, the man most knowledgeable about the *Herald* and the *Democrat,* for confirming that I have been fair in my analysis of these newspapers. During the preparation of my study, I was in closest rapport with U.S. Lesh. He had been a young lawyer in Huntington when Milligan was one of the oldest. U.S. Lesh, an eminent Republican lawyer and political leader, was the last of the lawyers directly inspired by Milligan's dedication to law. Fortunately, L. E. Carlson, the oldest Republican lawyer and political leader in Huntington, is in harmony with the thinking of U.S. Lesh.

Professors Bert Anson and Donald F. Carmony gave suggestions, and Dr. Lorna Lutes Sylvester provided superb help in the editing process for my "Lambdin P. Milligan's Appeal for States' Rights and Constitutional Liberty during the Civil War" in the *Indiana Magazine of History,* September, 1970. His Fort Wayne speech may be found there.

Many others have helped. I deeply appreciate their friendship, suggestions, and encouragement.

For this essay few of the sources have been cited except those that have to do with Milligan's own work. A list of primary and secondary sources would require another book. To achieve my purpose I have used space to give an explanation of motivation and I have related Milligan's fight against Lincoln to the big problems.

NOTES

1. Huntington, Indiana, *Herald,* December 22, 1899.
2. Those who want the lawyer's point of view are referred to Samuel Klaus, ed., *The Milligan Case* (New York, 1929). The contemporary military point of view was presented in Ben Pitman, ed., *The Trials for Treason at Indianapolis, 1864* (Cincinnati, 1865).
3. Huntington, Indiana, *News-Democrat,* March 29, 1898
4. Ibid.

MILLIGAN'S FIGHT AGAINST LINCOLN

Chapter I

Introduction

During the Civil War era, Lambdin P. Milligan lived just west of Huntington, Indiana, in a comfortable home. Serving as chairman of the Democrat party in Huntington County, he became prominent in the Eleventh Congressional District because of his fierce opposition to the policies of President Abraham Lincoln.[1]

The Northern Democrat opponent best known to Lincoln was Clement L. Vallandigham, a member of the United States Congress when Lincoln was elected president. As long as Lincoln lived, Milligan was simply grouped with those Democrats opposed to war to preserve the Union.[2] There was only one time, not long before Lincoln was assassinated, that he had occasion to know Milligan by name.

Because Milligan was nothing in national politics and not much more in state politics, political history has little about him. Even that little commonly accepts, as Allan Nevins did, much of the invective of Milligan's enemies.[3]

Milligan destroyed himself politically by refusing to accept what was politically possible. This gradually separated him from the leadership of the Democrat party and got him associated with extremists. Unfortunately for Milligan, enough in this group had unworthy motives to discredit all.

The piercing invective used by Milligan, and the probable results of such language, caused military authorities and Republican leaders to fear and to hate him.[4] In Huntington, long after the Civil War, the first thing remembered about Milligan was the fear.[5]

Fear, hatred, and association resulted in arrest and a trial by a military commission for Milligan along with others. Some took advantage of opportunities to escape; some made concessions to get released. Either escape or concessions satisfied their accusers, who considered this the final proof of guilt.

Partly because of the chance of timing, but to a large extent because of legal ability and intense legalism, Milligan's refusal to escape or to make concessions to lessen the probability of being hanged placed him in a class by himself. His fight against Lincoln was changed from the field of politics to the field of law. In the legal arena the fight was on equal terms. Both Milligan and Lincoln championed interpretations of law. The interpretation of Milligan was stronger from the standpoint of legal reason. The interpretation of Lincoln was stronger from the standpoint of practical government. Consequently Milligan had the help of lawyers as eminent as those who helped Lincoln.

Milligan's case got to the Supreme Court of the United States where he won a partial victory. But the basic question was not resolved: Should the Constitution of the United States be followed according to the intentions of those who drafted and ratified this fundamental law?

The legalism of Milligan which determined his affirmative stand, was in accord with a lifetime of law practice.[6] In his brief period of some importance in state politics, he was the most determined of the strict constructionists.[7]

However, it was on the basis of Lincoln's interpretation of the Constitution that the Union was preserved. Also it was on the basis of his interpretation that the United States became the greatest nation in the world.

NOTES

1. Emma Lou Thornbrough, *Indiana in the Civil War Era, 1850-1880* (Indianapolis, 1965), p. 216.
2. John G. Nicolay and John Hay, *Abraham Lincoln: A History,* 10 vols. (New York, 1890), pp. 328-395.
3. Allan Nevins, "The Case of the Copperhead Conspirator," in John A. Garraty, ed., *Quarrels That Have Shaped the Constitution* (New York, 1962), p. 92.
4. George Fort Milton, *Abraham Lincoln and the Fifth Column*

(New York, 1942), p. 308; Kenneth M. Stampp, *Indiana Politics during the Civil War* (Indianapolis, 1949), pp. 186-216.
5. Florence L. Grayston, "Lambdin P. Milligan: A Knight of the Golden Circle," *Indiana Magazine of History,* XLIII (1947), p. 379.
6. Huntington, Indiana, *News-Democrat,* December 26, 1899.
7. Gilbert Riley Tredway, *Indiana Against the Administration, 1861-1865,* Ph.D. dissertation (Indiana University, 1962), p. 232.

Chapter II

Decisions for Square Away

Throughout the entire world it is recognized that Abraham Lincoln was a great president of the United States. Only a few, mainly newspaper editors and lawyers, have recognized the heroic in Lambdin P. Milligan. The most appreciative analysis was made by Republicans and Democrats at the time of the death of Milligan.[1] Their conclusions were essentially substantiated in the careful study by U.S. Lesh, the last of the Republican lawyers directly inspired by Milligan.[2]

Local physical remains show the contrast in recognition. Milligan's home deteriorated and finally disappeared in 1964. A magnificent museum in Fort Wayne preserves the memory of Lincoln.[3] Nevertheless, the two men had important similarities. Indeed, what made compromise impossible was that they were similar in unshakable determination, and each had complete confidence in final victory.

The same Republican newspaper that during the Civil War most vigorously opposed Milligan later conceded that he was "a man of giant size and marked intellect. He was absolutely without affectation, kind-hearted, simple, approachable, dignified and courteous. He had, however, upon occasions, the power to exercise a blasting sarcasm. Whatever may be said by his political opponents of his career, all parties must admire his wonderful patience and unflinching courage when he was under the shadow of the gallows. Others charged with him ran off, turned state's evidence, hastened to explain and apologize, but he never wavered for a moment. . . ."[4]

The similarities of Milligan and Lincoln can partly be explained by similar experiences. Each had important differences

Decisions for Square Away

with his father and made a successful stand on his own, read law to become a lawyer instead of attending college where it would be necessary to adjust to the thinking of some professors, moved to the next state farther west, was physically tall, kept firm command based on respect, went through considerable failure, and had success in areas considered most important. Moreover, Milligan and Lincoln were railroad lawyers.

Dissimilar experiences help to explain unreconcilable positions. Milligan learned how to farm. After practicing law for ten years in Ohio, he moved to a farm in Huntington County. Although he moved close to Huntington when heavy demands were made on his time for law practice, he always kept an interest in farming.

Men whose early life was on the farm, and who later only kept an interest in farming, often have tended to be conservative. Therefore their thinking about the East has been similar to that of those who stayed on the farm and organized protest movements. Milligan's hostility to the East showed this, although he was mainly concerned about the corruption of law by the business interests located there.

Lincoln never returned to the farm. For political propaganda, skill with the axe was associated with his early life. Not nostalgia, but the search for a better way characterized his thinking and language.

Milligan was faithful to the Catholic Church and supported it generously. Although a deeply religious man, Lincoln was not a member of any church.

Lincoln had better health, more physical strength, and more ability to persuade. To get support as well as to discourage opposition, Milligan relied to a large extent on stimulating fear. Sometimes it was fear of the results of Lincoln's policies. At other times it was the fear of those in Democrat organizations. So great was this fear that Milligan was not distracted by any personal challenges. He did not even seem to be in any danger, yet in the area there were many fistfights and some were shot.

Because of different experiences, and different reactions to challenge, Milligan and Lincoln had an important dissimilarity. Milligan had strong tendencies to reject change. Lincoln, slowly and cautiously, tended to accept change. As these tendencies were applied to the constitutional problem in 1861, their positions became irreconcilable. It was not a matter of selfish ends and rationalizations to support them.

In 1861, the important change in law had to do with state sovereignty. Between 1787, when the Constitution of the United States was drafted, and 1861 no crisis was severe enough to force men to clarify what was meant by state sovereignty. Consequently Congress only debated and compromised.

Did state sovereignty, which gave each state the unquestioned choice to ratify or not ratify the Constitution, in Article VII, also mean that each state had a choice to leave the Union? To answer this question would include considering whether some reason, law, or political development controlled other than amendments provided for in Article V.

Before 1860 the answers to the question were found in the Tenth Amendment and judicial interpretation. On this basis one could either reject change except by amendment (Milligan) or support change in some lesser parts to preserve what was more important—the Union (Lincoln). The Tenth Amendment provided that "The powers not delegated to the United States by the Constitution, nor prohibited by it to the States, are reserved to the States respectively, or to the people." This recognizes the power of the state if it means the people of the state (Milligan). It grants the power to the central government that has a majority of all of the people if the word people refers to the people in all of the states (Lincoln).

Economic interests, especially agrarianism and industrialism, increased the confusion. Shifting political power that came from more rapid growth of population in the North infused rivalry, fear, and hatred into political thinking. One point of view (Lincoln's) became dominant in the North. There were those in the South, but no important leader, who agreed with this. Another point of view (Milligan's) was held by a determined minority in the North. Although this view was dominant in the South, no one in the South seems to have been aware of Milligan.

The points of view of both Lincoln and Milligan were based

on the thinking of Thomas Jefferson. As a political theorist Jefferson supported state sovereignty. However, when president of the United States, his action in the Louisiana purchase furthered the precedent for decisive control by the central government without an amendment to the Constitution.

Before Jefferson, the colonial charters were at the center of the controversy between the intent of the law when drafted and later change in practice. The charters, which provided the legal basis for the colonies, were granted by the king of England. At that time he had unquestioned authority to grant and to take away the grant. By 1776, no charter granted by the king or law passed by Parliament placed the colonies on a different basis. However, according to the Americans, the rights of Englishmen in the charters, the political theory of John Locke (d. 1704) and others, and American practice had become American liberty by 1776.

In 1776 the Americans claimed, and made good their claim, to the rights of life, liberty, and the pursuit of happiness. What the Americans meant by life and liberty was quite different from what the king had intended. Whatever the Americans had in mind by pursuit of happiness, at least it had not been granted by the king or included in a law passed by Parliament. To support the principle that justifies the American claim is to support the principle used by President Lincoln.

The victory of "change from practice" over the "intent of those who drafted the law" was not final for the Americans either in their theory or Constitution. The rights claimed were held to be inalienable. By definition, an inalienable right cannot be changed. Provision was made to change the Constitution, but only by amendment. Those who drafted the Constitution rejected the use of force against a state. No state that ratified showed any intent that force could legally be used to change its state sovereignty. The oath taken by the president of the United States as well as other officials was to "preserve, protect, and defend" the Constitution. No escape clause was inserted that permitted an official not to follow the law. Logically, to have liberty under law, the law must be obeyed. Consequently, as to support the principle that justifies the American claim in 1776 is to support Lincoln, so to support the principle that force could not be used to change what each state intended in 1787 is to support Milligan.

Lincoln's purpose when inaugurated president on March 4, 1861, was to uphold the law and to save the Union. In order to be as close as possible to the law, force was not used against any "state." Yet force was necessary to preserve the Union. Force was used against certain "people" in the South to require them to accept the decision of the majority of the people of the United States. This use of force against people who controlled a state was an interpretation Lincoln did not claim to be intended by those who drafted and ratified the Constitution. His claim was based on the proposition that he preserved and furthered two great purposes of the Constitution: a political organization best for economic growth, and a political organization that could defend itself.

Lincoln's firm stand to accept change was in accord with what he had decided as early as 1832: "I would not favor the passage of a law . . . , which might be very easily evaded. Let it be such that the labor and difficulty of evading it, could only be justified in cases of the greatest necessity . . . It is better to be only sometimes right, than at all times wrong, so as soon as I discover my opinions to be erroneous, I shall be ready to renounce them."[5]

To save the Union was such a "greatest necessity" for Lincoln. Civil War provided occasions to discover opinions to be "erroneous." Far from painting beautiful pictures of perfection resulting from change, Lincoln stressed what was preserved.

When opposing the extension of slavery, Lincoln followed the earlier practice successfully established by the Northwest Ordinance of 1787. On the specific point of arrests, Milligan recognized that Lincoln had three precedents that were sanctioned and affirmed by the legislature: the executive council in Pennsylvania, George Washington, and Andrew Jackson.[6]

Before Civil War accelerated change beyond compromise, Lincoln wrote a letter to Alexander H. Stephens of Georgia. Stephens kept the letter and published it after the war. The two thick volumes published by Stephens to prove that the Southern states were ever loyal and true to the Constitution[7] show how difficult it was to establish, even in the mind of the South, a convincing case against Lincoln.

Actually a convincing case in opposition to Lincoln was never achieved by southern politicians. Earlier, John C. Calhoun had worked out a better statement than that presented by Stephens.[8] Later, showing tenacity to preserve the old but also the impact of realism, Jefferson Davis was not as cogent as either Calhoun or Stephens.[9]

Confederate politicians inherited an enormous intellectual handicap because the South had supplied many of the leaders in 1776 who had accepted change in order to preserve liberty controlled by Americans. Moreover, as soon as the Southerners went from opposition—where theory was enough—to practice in their own organization where necessity had to be considered, change was accepted.

Consequently, if the theory of the South was closer to Milligan, the practice of the South was closer to Lincoln. The defeat of the South was hastened, if not caused, by not changing fast enough to end slavery and to have a strong central government to wage war. Men like Stephens had good reason to include a letter from Lincoln but not to mention Milligan. During the war the South was not interested in men in the North who championed the law, but in those who would break the law to help the South. After the war the South was not interested in theory only, but tried to show that correct theory was in accord with the Confederate practice. After the war, Milligan ceased to advocate theory; instead, consistent with a common practice of lawyers, he accepted the verdict.

The cautious position of Lincoln had much to offer those who thought in terms of practical politics. He simply stated that "in contemplation of universal law, and of the Constitution, the Union of these States is perpetual. Perpetuity is implied, if not expressed, in the fundamental law of all national governments."[10]

Unfortunately, when Lincoln became president the constitutional question was yoked with slavery. Earlier crisis, such as the War of 1812 and the tariff controversy, had not aroused such strong passions in the general public. Lincoln perfected the reasoning that supported the policy of perpetuity. He combined this reasoning with a serious call to cherish the spiritual life of the nation. But the "right" and "wrong" of slavery denied Lincoln the success of President Andrew Jackson in the preceding crisis when the tariff issue was compromised. Thus slavery was the only substantial dispute.[11]

The very word slave seethes with hatred and destroys reason and empathy. Probably the word was first used by those who hated the Slav people.

The Constitution of the United States, in Article IV, Section 2, stated that "No Person held to Service or Labour in one State, under the Laws thereof, escaping into another, shall in Consequence of any Law or Regulation therein, be discharged from such Service or Labour, but shall be delivered up on Claim of the Party to whom such Service or Labour may be due."

When the Constitution was drafted, hatred and confusion were not conjured by inserting the word "slave." The Thirteenth Amendment (December 18, 1865) shows the confusion that was only partly remedied by adding the more precise words "involuntary servitude." Slavery in the South was abolished. But slavery was permitted by the Amendment as punishment for crime. However, no punishment has been legally called slavery.

In 1860 many but not all of the blacks in the South were held by state law to service or labor. These blacks were in a different position from white people who were held in both the North and in the South to service or labor: blacks were held for an indefinite number of years; white people were held for a definite number of years. This difference had evolved from difficulties encountered during the colonial period.[12]

Provisions for blacks in the South had a colonial legal basis that was not clear. In England there had been no slaves and consequently no precedents. Lack of legal clarity in the South degenerated into rigid defense mechanisms nurtured by greed and race feeling.

Ignoring the practical political problem of slavery, which President Lincoln could not do, Milligan was convinced by evidence that is not easily discredited. His conclusion, that government by law is seriously weakened when precedents become established for not following the intent of those who drafted and ratified the Constitution, cannot be dismissed.[13]

Milligan's decision was in harmony with legalism but in contradiction with other interests he could have developed. Having been a colonel in the National Guard in Ohio before moving to Indiana, almost certainly he could have received a commission in the Union army. With a willingness to compromise legalism for what was politically expedient, almost certainly he could have been an important political leader. His opposition to the war meant personal financial loss. No personal danger, suffering, or loss ever caused Milligan to waver. Opposition, close at hand for Lincoln in 1861 and growing stronger as the war progressed, was in Congress. Using an interpretation of the Constitution much farther from strict construction than that of Lincoln, Congress conjured the theory of territorialization: States of the South had lapsed into the conditions of territories under the control of Congress.[14] This caused Lincoln to go in the direction of strict construction. Thus by the time Lincoln heard the name Milligan the two men had moved closer in their thinking about the Constitution.

NOTES

1. Huntington, Indiana, *News-Democrat*, December 21, 1899 and December 26, 1899; Huntington, Indiana, *Herald*, December 22, 1899.
2. Darwin Kelley, "U.S. Lesh: Lawyer and Leader, 1868-1965," *Indiana History Bulletin*, XLIII (May 1966).
3. Huntington, Indiana, *Herald-Press*, May 13, 1964; R. Gerald McMurtry "Fort Wayne Contacts with Abraham Lincoln," Public Library of Fort Wayne and Allen County (1966), p. 19.
4. *Herald*, December 15, 1899.
5. Roy Basler, ed., *The Collected Works of Abraham Lincoln*, 9 vols. (New Brunswick, 1954-1955), I:8.
6. *News-Democrat*, March 29, 1898.
7. Alexander H. Stephens, *A Constitutional View of the Late War*

Between the States, 2 vols. (Chicago, 1868-1870), II:50.
8. John C. Calhoun, *The Fort Hill Address of July 26, 1831* (Richmond, 1960).
9. Jefferson Davis, "Letter on States' Rights, June 20, 1885," *Southern Historical Society Papers* (1886), XIV: 409.
10. Basler, *Works of Lincoln,* IV:264. That, during the Civil War, the South was not interested in such men as Milligan and that Milligan was not interested in the South is a conclusion shared by Kinchen: Oscar A. Kinchen, *Confederate Operations in Canada and the North* (North Quincy, Mass.).
11. Ibid., IV: 269.
12. Edmund S. Morgan, "Slavery and Freedom: The American Paradox," *Journal of American History* (1972), LIX:7.
13. Virginia Commission on Constitutional Government, eds., *We the People* (Richmond, 1964), p. 404.
14. Herman Belz, *Reconstructing the Union: Theory and Practice during the Civil War* (Ithaca, 1969), p. 13.

Chapter III

Locale of Milligan

Milligan's defense of the intent of those who drafted and ratified the Constitution and Lincoln's acceptance of change would have resulted in a clash no matter where each lived. Nevertheless, how the conflict developed was influenced by the situation of each contestant. That of Lincoln is well known. Consequently only the situation of Milligan in Huntington, Indiana, needs to be described.

No state had a more energetic governor than Oliver P. Morton. Only four states had more presidential electors or members in the lower branch of Congress. Indiana had economic significance because of the production of hogs and wheat. Qualities of a pioneer community were still strong and intense pride, backed by determination, was characteristic of many. They established a reputation for being hardworking, patriotic, intelligent yeomen farmers and businessmen.[1]

More crucial aspects of the situation are not so clear. Neither at the time of the Civil War nor later has there been found a sure way to test assertions and denials. The "Indiana Democrats apparently believed that the war was unnecessary and would not have ensued except for the advent of the rival Republicans. By this time many Republicans believed, or at least pretended to accept the view, that a substantial element of the Hoosier Democracy would deliberately endanger the union or even bend to treason, if necessary, to defeat the Republicans."[2]

Huntington, the county seat of Huntington County, is about twenty-five miles southwest of Fort Wayne. A short distance west of Huntington the Wabash River has a branch called Little River that flows from the northeast through Huntington. In the early days Little River and swamps just west of Fort Wayne provided a way to go by canoe to Fort Wayne. This was the general route for later transportation and communication between Fort Wayne and points to the southwest. Thus the people in Huntington County looked to the East by way of Fort Wayne.

For several reasons many of the people in Huntington County, especially the Democrats, looked with more favor toward the South than toward the East. Some, both Republicans and Democrats, had migrated from the South. Trade tended to follow the Wabash River that flowed into the Ohio River and then into the Mississippi River.

Milligan not only shared these sentiments but also believed that those who controlled politics in the East debased the law. Although there were Democrats in Huntington County who disagreed with Milligan, they made no attempt to answer him. Instead, some joined the armed forces and provided later Democrats in the county with an honorable war record. Those Democrats concerned with the political leadership of Huntington County are still careful to point out that more Democrats than Republicans or Whigs joined the Union forces during the Civil War.[3] James R. Slack was the most prominent of these War Democrats and helped the Democrat party get reestablished after the war.[4]

Huntington County was far enough from the armed conflict that survival was not an immediate problem. But men serving in the armed forces and the popular absorption with politics made arguments deadly serious.

There were, of course, no slaves in Huntington County and only two free blacks in 1860.[5] Republicans tried to weaken the case of the Democrats by repeatedly assuring the people that the blacks would never come north. Democrats tended to concede this point and countered by asserting that abolitionists were a main cause of the war.[6] Sentiment on this problem favored the Democrats. A small stone building that was close to Milligan's home seems to be the only building in Huntington County remembered for its use as a place to keep blacks being returned to slavery in the South. However, contrary to what some thought, Milligan was not hostile to the blacks. What concerned him was that the law should be followed. Such things as race made no difference. It is

Locale of Milligan 17

remarkable how favorable the position of Milligan has proved to be for the blacks.

In 1861 there were in Huntington County few memories of military life. At the time of the Mexican War there had been only some six hundred voters and no company went from the county although some men enlisted.

The Indiana state constitution of 1850 provided that the militia should consist of all able-bodied white male persons between the ages of eighteen and forty-five.[7] In 1860 Huntington County had about twenty-five hundred men within those ages. Some eighteen hundred or nineteen hundred were eventually in the service.[8] With Republicans and War Democrats supporting the war, and Democrats supporting the soldiers while opposing the war, it was generally accepted that Huntington County did its full share. Bickering was over whether Republicans received more furloughs at election time in order to be able to vote. Colonel James R. Slack, a War Democrat, set the standard of patriotism. An incomplete list of men who lost their lives contains two hundred and seven names.[9] Thus almost one out of ten of military age lost his life.

Huntington County shared in the prosperity, as well as the military spirit. This furthered support for the Republicans.[10] Population increased from 1,565 in 1840, to 1,847 in 1850; to 14,865 in 1860, to 19,028 in 1870. Within the county the city of Huntington grew from 1,662 in 1850 to 2,925 in 1870; Antioch (Andrews) was not listed in 1860 but had 449 people in 1870; Roanoke grew from 270 in 1860 to 627 in 1870; Markle was not listed in 1860, but had 218 people in 1870; Warren grew from 228 in 1860 to 358 in 1870. The birthplaces in 1870 were: foreign, 1,200; Indiana, 10,474; Ohio, 4,657; Kentucky, 158; Pennsylvania, 1,150; Virginia and West Virginia, 292; and New York, 311.[11]

The cash value of farms in 1860 was $3,405,861. On these the main livestock consisted of horses, cattle, sheep, and hogs. The main crops were wheat, corn, and hay. The manufacturing establishments were similar to those in other parts of the state except that Huntington County had eight lime establishments. Products listed included lumber, flour, boots and shoes, agricultural implements, carriages, clothing, cooperage, furniture, iron castings, liquor, stone, printing, saddlery and harness, and shingles. The capital invested was $160,500 in 1860. By 1870 the capital invested was $451,710.[12]

A Republican newspaper, the *Herald,* edited by Alexander DeLong, and a Democratic newspaper, the *Democrat,* edited by Samuel F. Winter, fought tooth and toenail in every weekly issue. Each had four pages and was generous in the use of space for an appeal to a high level of intelligence. This stood in sharp contrast to a large amount of space used for scurrility.[13]

Both newspapers not only survived during the Civil War but also increased in vitality in spite of financial difficulties. The *Herald* had some advantage in more support from certain politically minded businessmen. At the beginning of the war they tried to ruin the *Democrat* by refusing to advertise and by stopping subscriptions. They were unsuccessful because most businessmen advertised wherever they could get good return on money spent.

Lawyers undergirded the editors and helped to keep the differences of opinion from generating hatred to the point of nothing but violence.[14] These lawyers bitterly opposed each other when they disagreed. They cordially worked together when they had a common goal.

It was because of the tenacity of Milligan's fight against Lincoln that the battle of ideas became of more than local importance. There was a "legacy of suppression" that had been established during the conflicts before 1800. The Common Law rule had been followed that criticism of the government (administration considered itself the government) was seditious libel. This legacy supported Lincoln. But also there was the First Amendment to the Constitution which in "unqualified and undefined terms"[15] provided constitutional law for the freedom of speech that became the rule in the comparatively united period after 1800. This constitutional law supported Milligan.

NOTES

1. Logan Esarey, "Pioneer Politics in Indiana," *Indiana Magazine of History* (1917), XIII: 286; William O. Lynch, "Indiana and Its History," *Indiana Magazine of History* (1943), XXXIX: 116; William B. Hesseltine, *Lincoln and the War Governors* (New York, 1948), p. 173.
2. John D. Barnhart and Donald F. Carmony, *Indiana from Frontier to Industrial Commonwealth*, 4 vols. (New York, 1954), II:155.
3. Ray Ade, "History of the Democratic Party in Huntington County," Huntington County Historical Society (1958), p. 5; Howard Houghton, "Huntington County Civil War Miscellany," Huntington County Historical Society (1960).
4. Frank Sumner Bash, *History of Huntington County, Indiana*, 2 vols. (Chicago, 1914), I:177-178.
5. U.S. Government, *Eighth Census of the United States, 1860*, 4 vols. (Washington, 1864-1866), I:106.
6. Emma Lou Thornbrough, "The Race Issue in Indiana Politics," *Indiana Magazine of History* (1951), XLVII:175.
7. Article XII, Section 1.
8. *Eighth Census, 1860*, I:106; Brant and Fuller, pubs., *History of Huntington County, Indiana* (Chicago, 1887), p. 364.
9. Ibid., pp. 364-370.
10. J. F. C. Fuller, *A Military History of the Western World*, 3 vols. (New York, 1954-1956), III:6; Avery O. Craven, "An Historical Adventure," *Journal of American History* (1964), LI:18.
11. U.S. Government, *Ninth Census of the United States, 1870*, 3 vols. (Washington, 1872), I:26, 125, 353. The population of Indiana was 1,350,428 in 1860. *Eighth Census, 1860*, I:106.
12. Ibid., II:38; *Ninth Census, 1870*, III:512, 657.
13. Thomas D. Clark, "The County Newspaper as a Source of Social History," *Indiana Magazine of History* (1952), XLVIII:232.
14. Deserters in Indiana, violence, and fear of violence kept the situation tense. Ella Lonn, *Desertion during the Civil War* (Gloucester, Massachusetts, 1966), p. 204.
15. Leonard W. Levy, *Freedom of Speech and Press in Early American History: Legacy of Suppression* (New York, 1963), ix, 309.

Chapter IV

Historical Background

The first part of this chapter will consider the historical background upon which Milligan relied. The latter part will consider the historical background upon which Lincoln relied. Milligan had the advantage of precedents, basing his reasoning on Magna Carta. President Lincoln had the advantage of what was best politically. Each can be defended because "For historical reasons the Constitution of the United States is both a political and a legal document. Under it, political questions are often legal and legal questions to some extent political."[1]

Milligan carefully distinguished between administration, the men in office, and government, the basic principles of the country.[2] From this standpoint, he was loyal to the government and opposed to the administration.

Theoretically, administration and government can be separated. In practice, especially in time of war, it is hard to draw a line. Democrats who opposed the administration were under a strain. Milligan was able simultaneously to remain opposed and to retain his loyalty because of his devotion to law. Those Democrats without something comparable were prone to rash actions that made tenable the accusation that they were traitors. Since in Indiana there was especially active and determined opposition to the Lincoln administration, the accusation that Democrats were traitors was especially insistent.[3]

Moreover, there was some truth to the charge that men opposing the administration were wily agitators who made it more difficult for men to do their duty. A cogent policy was requisite to win the war. Military men uniformly hold, as was done during the Civil war, that the war is right, that the administration is the government, that those who are loyal support administration.[4]

However, for those who follow John Locke, allegiance is

Historical Background

obedience according to law;[5] and for the men who drafted the Constitution of the United States, Locke and the earlier Sir Edward Coke were considered to have proper understanding of law. Coke was even more clearly on the side of Milligan than Locke. In the *Second Institute*, published in 1642, Coke stated that "no man can be taken, arrested, attached, or imprisoned but by due process of law, and according to the law of the land. . . ."[6]

Applicable to the situation in Indiana during the Civil War was the opinion of Sir Thomas Coventry a contemporary disciple of Coke, that those who were not soldiers were not subject to military law. When this was pointed out in England, the proposal to try civilians by martial law was dropped.[7]

A more popular interpretation was in the writing of Lord Macauley. He posited that one of the fruits of the Revolution of 1688-1689 was that "no man could be imprisoned, even for a day by the arbitrary will of the sovereign—no tool of power could plead the royal command as justification for violating any legal right of the humblest subject. They were held by both Whigs and Tories to fundamental laws of the realm."[8]

This constituted the English background of Milligan as it appeared in the *Democrat*. More often references were to the United States.

According to the review of American history in the *Democrat*, the colonies were distinct organizations. The Declaration of Independence continued this in state sovereignty.[9] Since the American Revolution was in opposition to the centralization of powers in Parliament, there were many provisions in the Declaration of Independence, the Articles of Confederation, the Constitution of the United States, and the state constitutions to establish the rights of each individual and each state. Moreover, "There was undoubtedly a strong and universal conviction among the men who framed and ratified the Constitution, that military force would not only be useless, but pernicious as a means of holding the States together."[10] At one time the interpretation of the Constitution in New England had been that the states should not be held together by force.[11]

It had been in order to avoid misunderstanding, asserted the

Democrat, that the Tenth Amendment was added, the general government being but a political agent of the states.[12] In accord with this, those who framed the constitution of Indiana were grateful to Almighty God, not the general government, for the right to choose their own form of government.[13]

The Fifth and Sixth amendments to the Constitution of the United States were quoted as clear evidence to support Milligan: "No person shall be held to answer for a capital, or otherwise infamous crime, unless on a presentment or indictment by a Grand Jury, except in cases arising in the land or naval forces, or in the Militia, when in actual service in time of War or public danger. . . . In all criminal prosecutions, the accused shall enjoy the right of a speedy and public trial, by an impartial jury of the State and district wherein the crime shall have been committed, which district shall have previously been ascertained by law, and to be informed of the nature and cause of the accusation . . . ."[14]

The warning of Patrick Henry was considered relevant: If your American chief be a man of ambition and abilities, how easy it is for him to render himself absolute!"[15] It was noted that the example of President George Washington was to separate civil and military authority; "constantly and strongly to impress upon the army that they were mere agents of civil power; that they have no more authority than other citizens; that offences against the laws are to be examined, not by a military officer, but by a magistrate; . . . that the whole country is not considered as within the limits of the camp."[16]

Thomas Jefferson, well known for his leadership,[17] was the authority most frequently resorted to by the *Democrat:* Jefferson believed that the general government was limited in its power over states, that the states should be supported, that as a last resort it was proper for the states to call a convention, and use force if necessary to preserve their rights. Moreover, Jefferson considered the Constitution to be defective because Congress had the power to suspend habeas corpus and never dreamed that the president had this power.[18] Jefferson expressed the feeling which was to have fresh meaning when Milligan was arrested in Huntington eighteen months after these words were quoted in the *Democrat:* "The

Historical Background

cowards who would suffer a countryman to be torn from their society in order to be thus offered a sacrifice to Parliamentary tyranny, would merit the everlasting infamy now fixed on the authors of the act."[19]

James Madison was usually merely included in the list with Washington, Jefferson, and Jackson. But sometimes Madison was cited by the *Democrat*. One reference was to maintain that people can live together in spite of differences.[20]

In his farewell address in March, 1837, President Andrew Jackson had charted the course that the *Democrat* considered should be followed. He rejected coercion: "If such a struggle is ever begun, and the citizens of one section of the country are arrayed against those of another in double conflict, let the battle terminate as it may, there will be an end to Union, and with it the end to the hope of freemen. The victory of the victors would not secure to them the blessings of liberty. It would avenge their wrongs, but they would themselves share in the common ruin."[21]

Other comments by Jackson were inserted from time to time. These affirmed that the abolitionists had the disloyal organization which, under the pretense of the love of freedom, promoted the dissolution of the Union; and that each state had the right to regulate its internal concerns. By following the advice of the old patriot, the *Democrat* believed that the country could have escaped the horrors of Civil War and instead been happy, united, and prosperous.[22]

Quotations from John Quincy Adams in the *Democrat* buttressed the position that it would be better to let the South go than to give military despotism a foothold in the government.[23]

The *Democrat* reasoned that had Daniel Webster been living his eloquence would have been heard against the usurpation of power by Lincoln. Webster would not have sanctioned the suspension of the Constitution.[24] He had denounced the infernal fanatics and abolitionists who strove to override the Constitution, defy the Supreme Court, and lay violent hands on those who disagreed with them.[25] Moreover, he had spoken for the ancient and undoubted prerogative of the people to canvas public measures and the merits of public men.[26]

Henry Clay, commented the *Democrat,* spoke the truth about the abolitionists. He had stated that for the abolitionists the right of property was nothing, the limitations on the central government were nothing, the powers of the states were nothing, and the dissolution of the Union was nothing.[27]

Although not in agreement with them at this time, the *Democrat* included in 1861 the speeches of former President James Buchanan and Senator Stephen A. Douglas. Buchanan declared that it was out of the question to recognize the independence of the South, that the Democrat Party should stop wasting time on futile peace propositions, and that until the South returned to the Union President Lincoln should be supported.[28] Douglas observed that compromise was no longer possible, that war was being waged, and that the path of duty for patriotic men was to support the flag as the only way to preserve the Union.[29]

Words of Douglas, who had passed through Huntington in October, 1860, and was introduced to a large enthusiastic crowd by James R. Slack, were long remembered and treated with respect. The same issue of the *Democrat* that contained the notice of the death of Douglas on June 3, 1861, also stated: "As the leader of the great National Democratic party and the elevated and far-seeing statesman, we have honored, loved, and revered his name; and though we may not have admired his many inconsistencies of late, yet we will none the less cherish his memory, for we believe that like our humble selves, the force of circumstances and the violent state of feeling in the North, consequent upon the assault on Fort Sumter, caused him to temporarily succumb, and to deviate from a straight-forward course to avoid the fury of the storm."[30]

The *Democrat* stayed with the "straight-forward" course: "The common remark of the day is, that all who think this war upon the South is a needless, unauthorized and unconstitutional war, are Traitors! While on the other hand there are those who honestly believe that Lincoln is a traitor to Constitutional Law, and a usurper of unauthorized powers. If those who entertain the latter opinion are in error, they have been led into that error by the Father of his Country, by the teachings of Jefferson and Jackson;

and by the speeches of eminent living statesmen. When we asserted, in our first article after the receipt of Lincoln's Proclamation, that he had no authority to call out troops, or to use them until authorized by Congress, we had just been reading the able and unanswerable speech of Judge Douglas, delivered in the Senate the 5th of March 1861."[31]

Three years later, after often repeated consideration, these convictions received a final form in the cadence of Milligan: "Mr. Douglas has said, 'He who, when his country is at war, stops to inquire whether she is right or wrong, is a traitor.' And others have said so before him; but I spurn it as the language of a courtier, and only fit to be made by hireling flatterers of power and is the vulgar acceptation of the phrase that 'the King can do no wrong.' The uniform American doctrine, both in theory and practice, has been that all aggressive wars are wrong. . . ."[32]

James R. Slack was the most important member of the Democrat party in Huntington County who disagreed with Milligan. For many years before the war Slack had been a local leader. At the beginning of the war he was in the state senate and was commended by the *Democrat*. However, Slack supported the war and was appointed by Governor Oliver P. Morton to be the colonel of the 47th Regiment. Slack's decision was to fight for the flag of Washington, the flag of Madison, the flag of Jackson, the flag "of our country—our whole country."[33]

By "mistake" an advertisement in the *Democrat* which praised Colonel Slack and urged other Democrats to volunteer appeared as an editorial. This was not set straight until three weeks later: It was an act of patriotism to accept the commission, but treason to democracy to levy war against the principles of the party and its members. For, "His course on the war question was dictated by a desire for office, and to be on the popular side. And we say further, that we believe that Gov. Morton gave him the appointment, not because of any fitness for the position, but because of his intense bitterness against his former political friends.[34]

Only rarely did Slack cross swords with Milligan. In the decisive face-to-face encounter at the county convention, Milligan's triumph was reported by the *Democrat:* "If we could have sympathy for one who has acted so false toward us, we could have pitied the General when Col. Milligan came down on his declaration that 'the Democratic party always was in favor of every war no matter by whom or for what purpose it was waged.' He said he knew that such was Mr. Slack's opinion of the Democratic party, for he had repeatedly heard him remark, after the call for volunteers by the President, that it was an 'unjust, unnecessary and abolition war, but that the Democratic party always was for war, and that the man who did not go in for the war would be politically crushed, and that we must all pitch in and take the wind out of the Republican sails.' He challenged Mr. Slack to deny saying so, and asserted that he was prepared to prove it by a host of witnesses. The General squatted, and looked like a clown's hat in the afterpiece of a circus. Col. Milligan repelled the charge as a foul slander upon the Democratic party; an insult to their intelligence to charge that they always would be in favor of war; to charge that they were incapable of discriminating between a just and an unjust war; to discriminate between a war waged in defense of the rights of our country, or in vindication of our country's honor, and a war illegally brought on by a Usurper, and for the furtherance of the ends of a foul fanatical abolition party."[35]

These were the precedents and political theories in Milligan's historical background that provided a strong respectable basis. Nevertheless, the practical point of view in the historical background of President Lincoln was much more compelling for the large majority of men in the North.

The survey of the controversy by Thomas M. Cooley gives the interpretation of history generally accepted in the North: "Besides the tie uniting the several colonies through the Crown of Great Britain, there had always been a strong tendency to a more intimate and voluntary union, whenever circumstances of danger threatened them; and this tendency led to the New England Confederation of 1643, to the temporary Congress of 1690, to the plan of union agreed upon in Convention in 1754, but rejected by the Colonies as well as the Crown, to the Stamp Act Congress of 1765, and finally to the Continental Congress of 1774. When the difficulties with Great Britain culminated in actual war, the

Historical Background

Congress of 1775 assumed to itself those powers of external control which before had been conceded to the Crown or to the Parliament, together with such other powers of sovereignty as it seemed essential a general government should exercise, and thus because the national government of the United Colonies. By this body, war was conducted, independence declared, treaties formed, and admiralty jurisdiction exercised. It is evident, therefore, that the States, though declared to be 'sovereign and independent,' were never strictly so in their individual character, but were always, in respect to the higher powers of sovereignty, subject to the control of a central authority, and were never separately known as members of the family of nations. The Declaration of Independence made them sovereign and independent States, by altogether abolishing the foreign jurisdiction, and substituting a national government of their own creation."[36]

From a different point of view, Alexis De Tocqueville observed that in the United States there was nothing really superior to the majority when it came to a final decision as to right. This was because the majority controlled public opinion, the legislature, the executive, the troops, and the judges.[37]

In 1830 and again in 1850 the practical heritage for which men in the North would live and die was envisioned by Senator Daniel Webster: "Liberty and Union, now and forever, one and inseparable!" And, "let us enjoy the fresh air of Liberty and Union . . . to grapple the people of all the States to this Constitution, for ages to come."[38]

In April 1861 the North was confronted with the imperative dilemma concealed in the words of Webster. As recognized by Hugh McCulloch from Fort Wayne, Indiana, who became prominent in Lincoln's administration, it was necessary to answer the fundamental question, whether a state had the right to withdraw from the Union.[39] That is, whether military power should be used to keep states from withdrawing. War Democrats, following the example of Senator Stephen A. Douglas, and Republicans (in other words the great majority in the North) became committed to military power.

Milligan's fight against Lincoln took place after the decision to use military power. Henry Adams accepted the result philosophically in 1870: The original basis of reserved powers for the states on which the Constitution was framed should yield to centralization of powers in the national government.[40] Legalism prevented Milligan from enjoying the satisfaction from such sentiments before, during, or after the war. He did not consider the problem that if, even for a short time, the American states were no longer one political organization, there was the prospect of constant war or threats of war, as in Europe.[41]

President Lincoln, although strong politically, had disadvantages from the standpoint of law. No matter how one interpreted the location of sovereignty when it changed from England to America, the thirteen states when colonies were a minority in the British Empire. Consequently the Constitution contained much that favored minority speaking and acting.

By 1864 Lincoln had established additional precedents. As soon recognized, although not placed into constitutional law until the ratification of amendments following the Civil War, the government of the United States was changed. There was no longer a federal union (states' rights). What emerged was a national government (centralized control on points considered important by the legislative, executive, and judicial branches in Washington).[42] How much of this was envisaged at the time of the American Revolution remains problematical. The language used was broad. The immediate main purpose was to rally the support of those who favored the independence of each colony which became a state. It may be that a farsighted few had the practical purpose to secure not the independence of each state but an independent nation.[43]

NOTES

1. Roscoe Pound, *The Development of Constitutional Guarantees of Liberty* (New Haven, 1957), p. 102; Maurice G. Baxter, *Daniel Webster and the Supreme Court* (Amherst, 1966), p. 245. There were many commentaries on the Constitution before 1860 and the ideas were well worked out, both the nationalist (loose construction) and the particularist (states' rights or strict con-

Historical Background

struction). There were strict constructionists in various parts of the Union, but the doctrine was commonly associated with the South.

Elizabeth Kelley Bauer, *Commentaries on the Constitution, 1790-1860* (New York, 1965), pp. 168, 211. The three commentators mentioned by Milligan in his Fort Wayne Speech were John Marshall, Joseph Story, and James Kent. He mentions them in such a way as to lessen their authority. The *Democrat* repudiated Jefferson Davis. *Democrat*, August 24, 1861. Conspicuously absent from the thinking of Milligan was any authority who gave support to the Confederacy.

2. Samuel Klaus, ed., *The Milligan Case* (New York, 1929), p. 417.
3. George Fort Milton, *Abraham Lincoln and the Fifth Column* (New York, 1942), p. 199; Morton Grodzins, *The Loyal and the Disloyal: Social Boundaries of Patriotism and Treason* (Chicago, 1956), p. 19.
4. W. H. H. Terrell, *Indiana in the War of the Rebellion: Report of the Adjutant General* (Indianapolis, 1960), p. 5. This is a reprint by the Indiana Historical Society of volume one of eight volumes published in 1869.
5. John Locke, *Two Treatises of Government: A Critical Edition with an Introduction and Apparatus Critique by Peter Laslett* (Cambridge, 1960), Second Treatise, Chapter XIII, p. 151.
6. Quoted in Pound, *The Development of Constitutional Guarantees of Liberty*, p. 156.
7. Huntington, Indiana, *Democrat*, January 22, 1863. Cited in the speech of Governor Horatio Seymour of New York, delivered to the legislature of New York on January 1, 1863. Coke's authority was not only usable for the main issue but also for relevant issues. In the *Institutes,* for example, a trial should be in the town where the inhabitants had the best and most certain knowledge of the facts. The *Reports* indicated that treason or felony should be sent to the King's Bench, not to the Tower. Edward Coke, *Institutes of the Laws of England or, a Commentary upon Littleton*, 2 vols. (Philadelphia, 1853), 125a; Lord Sanchar's Case in Coke, *Reports*, 13 parts (Dublin, 1792-1793), Part 9, pp. 117-118; Hastings Lyon and Herman Block, *Edward Coke, Oracle of the Law* (New York, 1929), p. 309.
8. *Democrat*, January 15, 1863.
9. Ibid., January 7, 1864; ibid., September 1, 1864. Although Bancroft supported reform and progress, he concluded in his last revision that during the American Revolution there was no distinction between the states in asserting the sovereignty of each separate state. George Bancroft, *History of the United States*

from the Discovery of the Continent to 1789, 6 vols. (New York, 1879), VI:174.
10. *Democrat,* November 5, 1863. Quotation from "the late Democratic Administration."
11. Ibid., May 30, 1861.
12. Ibid., May 14, 1863.
13. Ibid., January 7, 1864.
14. Ibid., October 13, 1864.
15. Ibid., August 15, 1861.
16. Ibid., August 6, 1863.
17. William O. Lynch, "Jefferson, the Liberal," *Indiana Magazine of History* (1944), XL:44.
18. *Democrat,* June 6, 1861; ibid., June 27, 1861; ibid., September 5, 1861; ibid., May 14, 1863; ibid., February 11, 1864.
19. Ibid., April 2, 1863; ibid., April 6, 1863.
20. Ibid., May 14, 1863. The citation was made to the *Federalist,* No. 14.
21. *Democrat,* April 4, 1861.
22. Ibid., June 27, 1861; ibid., September 19, 1861; ibid., May 14, 1863; ibid., May 10, 1864.
23. Ibid., April 30, 1863. Citation to Adams, April 30, 1839.
24. *Democrat,* January 9, 1862. Reference to Webster in 1851-1852. Webster only went so far as to favor broad construction of the Constitution as entrusted to the Supreme Court. Maurice G. Baxter, *Daniel Webster and the Supreme Court* (Amherst, 1966), p. 241.
25. *Democrat,* April 30, 1863.
26. Ibid., May 14, 1863.
27. *Democrat,* February 26, 1863; ibid., May 21, 1863.
28. Ibid., October 17, 1861; Philip Shriver Klein, *President James Buchanan: A Biography* (University Park, 1962), p. 416.
29. *Democrat,* June 6, 1861.
30. Ibid., June 6, 1861; ibid., October 4, 1860.
31. Ibid., June 6, 1861.
32. Ibid., September 1, 1864. Fort Wayne speech delivered August 13, 1864.
33. Huntington, Indiana, *Herald-Press,* June 25, 1961. Reprint of Slack's speech when a flag was presented to the regiment by the ladies of Wabash County.
34. *Democrat,* October 3, 1861; ibid., October 24, 1861. Quotation is from October 24, 1861.
35. Ibid., August 15, 1861.
36. Thomas M. Cooley, *A Treatise on the Constitutional Limitations Which Rest Upon the Legislative Power of the States of the*

Historical Background

American Union (Boston, 1890), pp. 7-8; probably the most succinct statement was in the letter of the Constitutional Convention to Congress, a letter signed by George Washington: "It is obviously impracticable in the federal government of these states, to secure all rights of independent sovereignty to each, and yet provide for the interest and safety of all." Quoted in Bauer, *Commentaries*, pp. 215-216.

37. Alexis de Tocqueville, *Democracy in America*, 2 vols. (New York, 1899), I:278.
38. Daniel Webster, *Writings and Speeches,* 18 vols. (Boston, 1903), VI:75; X:97; Baxter, *Daniel Webster and the Supreme Court,* p. 241.
39. Hugh McCulloch, *Men and Measures of Half a Century* (New York, 1888), p. 163; John D. Barnhart, "The Impact of the Civil War on Indiana," *Indiana Magazine of History* (1961), LVII: 185.
40. Henry Adams, "A Changed Government," in William B. Hesseltine, ed., *The Tragic Conflict: The Civil War and Reconstruction* (New York, 1962), p. 127.
41. Benjamin P. Thomas and Harold M. Hyman, *Stanton: The Life and Times of Lincoln's Secretary of War* (New York, 1962), p. 229.
42. Hermann Edward von Holst, *The Constitutional and Political History of the United States,* 8 vols. (Chicago, 1889-1892), VII:284.
43. Merrill Jensen, *The Founding of a Nation: A History of the American Revolution, 1763-1776* (New York, 1968), pp. 486, 515, 613, 703.

Chapter V

Change Accepted by Lincoln, 1861-1862

President Lincoln was convinced that the Union should be preserved. Under the pressure of what he believed was absolute necessity, some of his acts were questionable from the standpoint of the rule of law. These acts were marked by caution and restraint. Emphasis was given to what was preserved.

Nevertheless, the use of precedents by executives was beyond the power of Lincoln. The "bar of history" that came to support Lincoln had such qualifications as that his case was unique and that the American people's sense of constitutional government was not changed.[1]

In short, Lincoln was vulnerable to the attack by Milligan. But this vulnerability was limited to the arena of law. Meanwhile, Lincoln secured political and military victory: The Union was preserved. From the standpoint of politics, "we can see how right, and even inevitable, were the conclusions to which Lincoln found his way. . . . Because he had been elected by all the people he must, even without the consent of Congress or Court, do what was necessary."[2]

The later a person was born in the twentieth century, the more effort it will probably take to realize the patriotic emotions in the North that supported President Lincoln after April 1861. These patriotic emotions enabled him to keep political support when he accepted change to save the Union. This developed from his concept of American law stated in 1832.[3] It was in accord with the legal philosophy which held that law should achieve the goals of the nation.[4]

President Lincoln took steps to hold the allegiance of the Republican party plus those outside the party who supported the Union. As soon as possible he used patronage.[5] Many Democrats were officers in the armed forces.

After eight years in the Illinois legislature[6] and two years in the United States House of Representatives, Lincoln realized "No policy that does not rest upon some philosophical public opinion can be permanently maintained."[7] In February 1861 Lincoln stopped at Indianapolis and said: "with you, is the question, 'Shall the Union and shall the liberties of this country be preserved to the latest generation?' "[8]

Lincoln reasoned in his first inaugural address (March 1861) that the decision of the majority should be accepted. He knew that to have a majority required the support of many who were not Republicans. There was opposition in the cabinet to a war to preserve the Union. The constitutional right of coercion by a government upon a seceded state was disputed by most Democrat leaders and many Republicans when the South fired upon Fort Sumter in April 1861. After this, in the North, there was enthusiasm for preserving the Union. By July 1861 President Lincoln believed Union men were a majority even in many, if not all, of the "so-called" seceded states.[9]

What made it difficult to hold the allegiance of the majority was the change necessary to save the Union. That Lincoln preferred not to change was stated in his speech in New York City in February 1861: "I hope to feel no necessity pressing upon me to say anything in conflict with the constitution, in conflict with the continued union of these States—in conflict with the perpetuation of the liberties of these people. . . ."[10]

However, after hostilities began in April 1861, President Lincoln did what he had hoped not to do. On April 21, 1861, he advanced two million dollars of government money.[11] In May he called for volunteers and made large additions to the regular army and navy.[12] This was done because "no choice was left but to call out the war power of the Government. . . . These measures, whether strictly legal or not, were ventured upon, under what appeared to be a popular demand, and a public necessity; trusting, then as now, that Congress would readily ratify them. . . . It was with the deepest regret that the Executive found the duty of employing the war-power. . . ."[13]

Arbitrary arrests, the point that later involved Milligan personally, were also considered necessary. Yet Lincoln was reluctant: "Unless the necessity for these arbitrary arrests is manifest, and urgent, I prefer they should cease."[14]

In his message to Congress on July 4, 1861, Lincoln considered the problem in more detail: "Soon after the first call for militia, it was considered a duty to authorize the Commanding General, in proper cases, according to his discretion, to suspend the privilege of the writ of habeas corpus; or, in other words, to arrest, and detain, without resort to the ordinary processes and forms of law, such individuals as he might deem dangerous to public safety. This authority has purposely been exercised but very sparingly. Nevertheless, the legality and propriety of what has been done under it, are questioned; and the attention of the country has been called to the proposition that one who is sworn to 'take care that the laws be faithfully executed,' should not himself violate them. Of course some consideration was given to the question of power, and propriety, before this matter was acted upon. The whole of the laws which were required to be faithfully executed, were being resisted, and failing of execution, in nearly one-third of the States. Must they be allowed to finally fail of execution, even had it been perfectly clear, that by the use of the means necessary to their execution, some single law, made in such extreme tenderness of the citizen's liberty, that practically, it relieves more of the guilty, than of the innocent, should, to a very limited extent, be violated? To state the question more directly, are all the laws, but one, to go unexecuted, and the government itself go to pieces, lest that one be violated? Even in such a case, would not the official oath be broken, if the government should be overthrown, when it was believed that disregarding a single law, would tend to preserve it? But it was not believed that this question was presented. It was not believed that any law was violated. The provision of the Constitution that 'The privilege of the writ of habeas corpus shall not be suspended unless when, in cases of rebellion, or invasion, the public safety may require it,' is

Change Accepted by Lincoln

equivalent to a provision—is a provision—that such privilege may be suspended when, in cases of rebellion, or invasion, the public safety does require it. It was decided that we have a case of rebellion, and that the public safety does require a qualified suspension of the provision of the writ which was authorized to be made. Now it is insisted that Congress, and not the Executive, is vested with this power. But the Constitution itself, is silent as to which, or who, is to exercise the power; and as the provision was plainly made for a dangerous emergency, it cannot be believed the framers of the instrument intended, that in every case, the danger should run its course, until Congress could be called together; the very assembling of which might be prevented, as was intended in this case, by the rebellion."[15]

Lincoln continued during the war to support arrest, detention, and trial by the military. However, by June 1863, there was the position of Judge David Davis, a judge appointed by Lincoln, that there should not be punishment by court-martial for civilians.[16] Of course Lincoln reviewed trials by court-martial.

Also in connection with slavery President Lincoln accepted change. In March 1860 he stated: "I do not say that we would or should meddle with it where it exists; but we could inaugurate a policy which would treat it as a wrong, and prevent its extension."[17] Lincoln stressed that he was against "extension."

This was defended as in accord with the Constitution: "In all matters but this of Slavery the framers of the Constitution used the very clearest, shortest, and most direct language. . . . Only one reason is possible and that is supplied by one of the framers of the Constitution—and it is not possible for man to conceive of any other—they expected and desired that the system should come to an end, and meant that when it did, the Constitution would not show that there had ever been a slave in this good free country of ours."[18]

By March 1862 President Lincoln was urging the gradual abolition, with compensation, of slaves in the border states.[19] But General John C. Fremont's "proclamation, as to confiscation of property, and the liberation of slaves, is purely political, and not within the range of military law, or necessity."[20] A year later, as commander in chief of the army and navy, President Lincoln assumed that he had authority because "I suppose I have a right to take any measure which may best subdue the enemy."[21] His Emancipation Proclamation was in September 1862.

In 1862 many Democrats were elected. As President Lincoln stated, "the ill-success of the war had much to do with this."[22] However Congress was controlled by Union men, Republicans and War Democrats.

The situation in Indiana was not so favorable for Republicans. Democrats who did not support the war, at least in a way acceptable to Governor Morton and War Democrats, were in control of the Indiana state legislature. Of course this affected Huntington County.[23] Milligan had a better opportunity to oppose Governor Morton and President Lincoln. This exacerbated Milligan's relationship with the military authorities[24] and with Alexander DeLong,[25] editor of the *Herald,* who brought the principles of Lincoln into direct conflict with Milligan.

DeLong was well established in the community as a man of positive convictions with the integrity to stand for what he considered right. He was a man of quick practical intelligence, fair-minded, humane, a tolerant Catholic, and wrote with fiery personal convictions for a cause in which his father served as an officer and a brother was killed.[26]

DeLong's task was indicated early in the war: "Nothwithstanding the fact that our little county enjoys the reputation abroad of having within its limits more traitors than any other one north of the National road, we are much gratified in being able to state that she will do her duty in furnishing men to aid in the preservation of the Government."[27]

With news stories and editorials he stimulated the home support much desired by the army.[28] He could report that the "mass of our people are loyal, and feel a proper interest in the enforcement of the laws and the preservation of the Government."[29]

As for the traitors within Huntington County, "There are a

few individuals about town—and we rejoice to know that the number is small—who are laboring pretty hard to attract public attention by expressing deep sympathy for the thieves and traitors who are striving to break up the Union."[30]

The traitors who bothered the *Herald* the most were those associated with the *Democrat*. Each "man who gives aid and comfort to the enemies of his country by finding fault with his Government for resisting treason with its strong military arm, and keeps up a constant howling for compromise with traitors, and thereby throws obstacles in the way of the Government in its efforts to vindicate its honor, is as much of a traitor, morally, as the man who leads the rebel army, and, indeed, does his country more harm. The editors of the Huntington *Democrat* are traitors. . . ."[31]

Soon DeLong accepted the position of Governor Morton that those guilty of treason should be searched out and punished.[32] Although much of this invective was a mask to stimulate popular support in a rough society, yet words were never far from acts to carry them out. Violent action was often restrained by President Lincoln who did not use invective.

The tone was set in Huntington County by Isaac DeLong, father of the editor, who was serving in Virginia: "If there are any of the rebel tribe in Huntington county it is the duty of loyal citizens to destroy them as they would rattlesnakes. . . ."[33]

Only Milligan among the Democrats found invective that stung as much as that of the Republicans. Part of the explanation for Milligan almost being the first man executed for opposition to the war is that those in authority were angered by his thrusts.

Milligan directed his invective toward army officers, Governor Morton, and President Lincoln. It was left to the editor of the *Democrat,* Samuel F. Winter,[34] to denounce DeLong: "We have heard of mean men, of suck-egg dogs, of white-livered cent-skinning, hell-deserving scoundrels, of Abe Lincoln, Bill Seward, Simon Cameron, William Lloyd Garrison, Wendell Phillips, L. B. Chamberlain, Joshua R. Giddings, of the fellow in France who used to seduce women and then kill them, of John A. Murrill, the land pirate, of John Brown; but all these epithets are tame, and men named are gentlemen in comparison with the shame-faced skunk who publishes the Huntington *Herald*."[35]

Commenting on the fact that the "skunk" was of military age but not in uniform, it was suggested that "Removed from all danger, and he is very brave; but let danger threaten and he is not the man to brave it."[36]

But the editor of the *Herald* wrote off these words and many more as "true to his disloyal instincts."[37] Milligan continued to advertise in the *Herald* as well as the *Democrat* and the *Herald* to some extent maintained the policy announced in the first issue: "our course toward our political opponents, shall ever be mild, courteous, and gentlemanly; and we will endeavor to avoid, at all times, the abusive language which characterizes so many of the political papers of the present day."[38]

Throughout the war DeLong used persuasion by emphasizing the facts and interpretations that strengthened President Lincoln. DeLong searched history and mined the writings of authorities. He called attention to the inadequacies of the South, such as the smaller population.[39] He rejected peaceable separation. He praised those Democrats who would fight to prevent secession.[40]

He noted that when threatened by Shay's Rebellion, George Washington had advised the use of force,[41] and that Andrew Jackson had been outspoken against rebels and traitors. DeLong considered the policy of Lincoln to be almost identical with that of Jackson when, in relation to South Carolina in 1833, his proclamation stated that the "Constitution of the United States forms a government in which all the people are represented." For De Long this meant "To say that any state may at pleasure secede from the Union, is to say that the United States are not a nation. . . . An attempt by force of arms to destroy a government is an offense, and such government has a right, by the law of self-defense, to pass acts for punishing the offender."[42]

DeLong considered the proposal for a Northwestern Confederacy to be "silly and contemptible," an insult to the great body of honest Democrats.[43] With the outbreak of the "long

Change Accepted by Lincoln

threatened storm" all men were urged to throw aside party feeling and support the government.[44] This was at the time when Huntington County was sharing in the surge of patriotism.[45] Stephen A. Douglas, who had called upon all "true and loyal citizens to rally in support of the Constitution and laws,"[46] was quoted repeatedly.

"During the war of the Revolution," observed DeLong, "there was a self-styled Peace Party in the United States. The members thereof, truthfully remarks a cotemporary, were denominated Tories. They insisted on the inadequacy of the wrongs suffered by the colonists to justify a resort to arms; insinuated that the colonists had provoked the severities of which they complained. . . . There was a Peace Party during the war of 1812. The members of it were called Federalists. . . . They held a famous Peace Meeting at Hartford and the result was that all the men who participated in that convocation were consigned to an immortality of shame. There is a Peace Party in the country now. . . . They have inherited all of the vices and none of the virtues of both Tories and Federalists."[47]

With those in the Peace party in mind, DeLong quoted George Washington on traitors: "Why should persons, who are preying upon the vitals of their country, be suffered to stalk around while we know they will do us every mischief in their power?"[48]

By 1862 the first enthusiasm that supported the war had dissipated. DeLong gave more attention to justification for silencing or making impotent opposition to the war. He called upon the Democrats to read carefully such provisions of the Constitution of the United States as that treason included "adhering" to the enemies of the United States.[49] Those nominated by the Democrats for the election in October were traitors because "This ticket, with perhaps a single exception, is thoroughly Secesh, and is better adapted to the Southern latitude than this. That it will meet with the same fate that usually overtakes the armed forces of the South, we entertain not a particle of doubt."[50]

However, it was beyond the power of DeLong to prevent the failure of the Union army in July in front of Richmond from showing that in fact there was reason for doubt. The Northern armies "in some degree, lost their prestige. They had not only been defeated but out-generaled, which humiliated and discouraged the troops in the field, and materially detracted from that enthusiasm which was so needful to encourage recruiting at home."[51]

Consequently Milligan's opposition to the war became almost unbearable for DeLong. His reaction was bitter! "None can compare in traitorous malignity and falsehood to the one hissed forth from the villainous lips of L. P. Milligan." Statements of Milligan quoted to prove this included " 'no hope for the Union . . . we have not a friend in the East. . . . Deluded soldiers . . . sacrificed their lives on the altar of folly. . . . Tack the West on as the tail of a kite to New England. . . .' " But Milligan did not utter "a single word in opposition to treason or disunion."[52] Moreover, Milligan accused the "President and Cabinet with doing more to prolong the war than the rebels themselves, and consequently were worse than rebels."[53]

DeLong became grim: "It is about time that people understood that this war is to be one of submission or extermination. . . . Either one or the other—the North or the South—must be conquered by the hardest kind of warfare before this contest is ended. We have no mercy to expect from the secession barbarians, and none to offer until they throw down their arms and surrender their wicked leaders into the hands of justice."[54]

Senator Joseph A. Wright, a War Democrat who supported the Union party in 1862, made a speech in Huntington that De Long appreciated. Wright went so far as to assert that "this is no time to hesitate, put it in the hands of every officer throughout the North . . . that a man who is not for this Union must forfeit all he has." When asked whether he would make a military officer the judge of the loyalty of the citizens, Wright replied: "I would not make a military officer the judge of a man's conscience, but we can always tell men by their acts. We have a great many men furnishing aid and comfort to the South. We have men all over the North who cannot see anything right in this war. I would make every military commander my officer, I would lay down my rule . . . and then I would let the court determine the question."[55]

In accord with these ideas DeLong approved the arrest of Dr. T. Horton by the United States Marshal of Indiana. Horton lived

Change Accepted by Lincoln

in Bluffton which is in Wells County just east of Huntington County. He was "an unprincipled, foul-mouthed politician and an out-and-out rebel sympathizer." The confederates of Horton should also be arrested, imprisoned, and detained "until the flesh falls from their traitorous bones."[56] In this statement DeLong went much further than important Republican judges, especially David Davis. Judge Davis took the position that indictment and trial according to the Constitution should precede punishment.[57]

Also generating much heat in Huntington County for the October election was the race problem. In answer to the charge by the *Democrat* that more Negroes would come to Indiana, the *Herald* replied that "We have laws prohibiting it and these will be rigidly enforced."[58]

In the October elections the Democrats won in Huntington County. In November the Democrats carried the state.

In October 1862 DeLong contended that the South should have accepted the result of the election in 1860 and that "This war is to establish the right of the people to govern."[59] But in November 1862 a four-column statement by A. H. Conner, chairman of the state Union Central Committee made the charge that the election was carried by fraud.[60] This statement presaged the refusal of the Republicans, whose governor continued in office two more years, to actually permit the Democrats (the majority) to control in the state after winning the election of 1862. DeLong shifted from "the right of the people to govern" to admiration for President Lincoln: "there lives no loyal American who distrusts his earnest desire to serve and save the Union."[61]

NOTES

1. James G. Randall, *Lincoln: The Liberal Statesman* (New York, 1947), pp. 123, 133. According to Roche, the administration of Lincoln provided the first full display of nonconstitutional and nonstatutory authority applied to domestic emergency. John P. Roche, *Shadow and Substance: Essays on the Theory and Structure of Politics* (New York, 1964), pp. 134, 138. According to one closer to Lincoln, Von Holst, not to have preserved the

Union would have been the greatest attack on civilization recorded in the history of the world. Hermann Edward von Holst, *Constitutional and Political History of the United States,* 8 vols. (Chicago, 1876), VII:293.
2. Rexford G. Tugwell, *The Enlargement of the Presidency* (New York, 1960), p. 157.
3. See the quotation from Lincoln on this problem in Chapter I.
4. Samuel P. Huntington, *The Soldier and the State: The Theory and Politics of Civil-Military Relations* (Cambridge, 1957), p. 179; James Willard Hurst, *Law and the Conditions of Freedom in the Nineteenth-Century United States* (Madison, 1956), p. 5.
5. Harry J. Carman and Reinhard H. Luthin, *Lincoln and the Patronage* (New York, 1943), p. 332.
6. Paul Simon, *Lincoln's Preparation for Greatness: The Illinois Legislative Years* (Norman, 1965), p. 290.
7. Roy Basler, ed., *The Collected Works of Abraham Lincoln,* 9 vols. (New Brunswick, 1953-1955), IV:17; William H. Seward, *Works,* 5 vols. (New York, 1853-1884), V:195.
8. Basler, *Works of Lincoln,* IV:231.
9. Ibid., IV:268, 437; Gideon Welles, *Selected Essays* (New York, 1959-1960), p. 36; A. K. McClure, *Lincoln and Men of War Times* (Philadelphia, 1962), p. 260.
10. Basler, *Works of Lincoln,* IV:231.
11. Ibid., p. 242.
12. Ibid., p. 354.
13. Ibid., pp. 426, 429, 440.
14. Ibid., p. 372.
15. Ibid., pp. 429-431.
16. Willard L. King, *Lincoln's Manager: David Davis* (Cambridge, 1960), pp. 247-249.
17. Basler, *Works of Lincoln,* IV:5.
18. Ibid., p. 22.
19. Ibid., pp. 144-145, 317.
20. Ibid., p. 531.
21. Ibid., V:421. This confiscation of property without compensation in time proved to be the part of the Northern victory most acceptable to the South. Clement Eaton, *The Waning of the Old South Civilization, 1860-1880's* (Athens, 1968), p. 171.
22. Basler, *Works of Lincoln,* V:494.
23. Ray Ade, *History of the Democratic Party in Huntington County* (Huntington County Historical Society, 1957), p. 5; William Gordon, *History of the Republican Party in Huntington County* (Huntington County Historical Society, 1957), p. 7.
24. The military department that included Indiana was constituted

Change Accepted by Lincoln

May 3, 1861, under General Order No. 14, Adjutant General's Office, War Department. W. H. H. Terrell, *Indiana in the War of the Rebellion: Report of the Adjutant General* (Indianapolis, 1960), p. 555. This is a reprint of Volume I of the eight-volume report published in 1869.
25. Little is known about DeLong. The longest account is in the Huntington, Indiana, *Herald-Press*, January 2, 1964. Born in 1828, he had been editor of the *Herald* since it began in 1848. Darwin Kelley, *The Challenge of the Frontier at the Forks of the Wabash in 1848* (Indiana Historical Bureau, 1962).
26. Huntington, Indiana, *Herald*, November 30, 1864.
27. Ibid., September 4, 1861. The county with the highest number of volunteers was Wabash with 134. Huntington County was second with 104, and Wells was third with 102. Terrell, *Indiana in the War of the Rebellion*, p. 132.
28. Benjamin P. Thomas, ed., *Three Years with Grant, as Recalled by War Correspondent Sylvanus Cadwallader* (New York, 1955), pp. vii, 111.
29. *Herald*, September 4, 1861.
30. Ibid., May 8, 1861.
31. Ibid., July 31, 1861.
32. Ibid., August 28, 1861.
33. Ibid., October 9, 1861.
34. Even less is known about the editor of the *Democrat* than about the editor of the *Herald*.
35. Huntington, Indiana, *Democrat*, May 8, 1862.
36. Ibid., September 11, 1862. Exemption of DeLong for "deafness" was considered a political excuse since, according to the *Democrat*, DeLong could attend a public meeting and report the remarks of the speaker.
37. *Herald*, February 11, 1863.
38. Ibid., July 5, 1848.
39. Ibid., February 27, 1861.
40. Ibid., March 6, 1861.
41. Ibid., March 13, 1861.
42. Ibid., April 3, 1861.
43. Ibid., April 10, 1861.
44. Ibid., April 24, 1861.
45. Alan T. Nolan, *The Iron Brigade: A Military History* (New York, 1961), p. 33; Logan Esarey, *History of Indiana from Its Exploration to 1922*, 4 vols. (Dayton, Ohio, 1924), II:738.
46. *Herald*, May 1, 1861.
47. Ibid., September 25, 1861.
48. Ibid., October 9, 1861.

49. Ibid., April 30, 1862.
50. Ibid., June 18, 1862.
51. Terrell, *Indiana in the War of the Rebellion,* p. 22.
52. *Herald,* August 6, 1862.
53. Ibid., August 6, 1862; August 13, 1862.
54. Ibid., August 27, 1862.
55. Ibid., October 1, 1862.
56. Ibid., October 22, 1862.
57. Willard L. King, *Lincoln's Manager: David Davis* (Cambridge, 1960), p. 248.
58. *Herald,* October 22, 1862.
59. Ibid., October 22, 1862.
60. Ibid., November 26, 1862.
61. Ibid., December 10, 1862.

Chapter VI

Change Resisted by Milligan, 1861-1862

Because of the leadership that was provided by President Abraham Lincoln,[1] and the scorn many in the North had for those with unworthy motives who opposed the war,[2] Lambdin P. Milligan was politically doomed. Nevertheless, there were men in the North as well as the South who were devoted to states' rights in 1860.[3] Also, prominent Republicans as well as Democrats had little confidence in Lincoln as late as February 1861.[4]

In Huntington County the lack of confidence in Lincoln nurtured the alluring notion that peaceable secession, which might result in early reconstruction, was preferable to civil war when the constitutional right of coercion was doubtful. This situation lasted until the South fired on Fort Sumter. Then wavering Republicans, and Democrats who came to be called War Democrats, changed to support preserving the Union by force. Milligan became the leader of those who did not change.

The epithet "'Copperhead," meaning snake, got firmly fixed on the Democrats who opposed President Lincoln. This "stung like a lash."[5] It persisted to discredit those who opposed the war.[6] Copperhead was applied to Milligan although his relationship with Democrat leaders was tenuous. Before 1864 Milligan was known throughout the state as a lawyer.[7] Only the *Democrat* published everything that might further his cause and not even this was without friction. The *Democrat* in 1861 was edited by William C. Kocher and Samuel F. Winter. Winter did most of the writing and with tenacious loyalty upheld Milligan. Kocher responded more to political expediency and disposed of his interest in the newspaper in 1863.[8] It is still difficult to consider the Democrats during the Civil War without becoming emotionally involved in the party split that racked the editors.[9]

Not until the Civil War was over did Milligan receive important support from lawyers who opposed exercise by the president of absolute power.[10] By that time the United States was market-focused and was more concerned with prosperity.[11]

Before 1850 Huntington County had been Democrat.[12] However, in 1860 there were 1,604 votes for Lincoln, 1,402 for Douglas, and 54 for Breckinridge. After the South Carolina Ordinance of Secession in December 1860, the Democrats in Huntington County were thrown into confusion, as they were throughout Indiana.[13]

The *Democrat* on December 27, 1860, stated that the right of secession was one of the reserved rights of the states. One week later, on January 3, 1861, it declared that those who cried disunion were traitors. The next week there was a statement that the senior editor, Kocher, on January 3 not only "did not coincide with us" but also "took direct grounds against us."[14]

This marked also the split in the local Democrat party leadership. Milligan and James R. Slack had both spoken in favor of Douglas in June 1860. Slack, who had much more political ability, changed with Douglas.

Further confusing the situation for Milligan was the example of John C. Breckinridge. This Democrat from Kentucky was best known as one of the defeated candidates for President in 1860. In 1861 he was a United States Senator who opposed President Lincoln on the grounds of constitutionality. He was expelled from the Senate and became an officer in the Confederate army. Thereafter, any man who spoke of constitutionality, as Milligan did, was taunted as being a "Southerner" who should join his "friends." This stuck to Milligan until his death, and long afterwards.[15]

Moreover, when the entire war period is considered, Milligan had more points of friction than ties of unity with the most prominent Democrat who opposed Lincoln, Clement L. Vallandigham. He was an idealist.[16] Yet when a practical decision was made by the Democrat Party, Vallandigham could support the party. Milligan was a legalist. He kept working on what was in-

Change Resisted by Milligan

tended by the law and finally presented his complete statement in the Fort Wayne Speech in 1864. When the Democrat party rejected his ideas, he would not change.

An early statement by Milligan was in the majority report of the Union meeting that included Republicans and Democrats from Huntington County. Isaac DeLong spoke in favor of a minority report that supported President Lincoln. Of course this was also the point of view of his son, Alexander DeLong.[17] Within two weeks came the report of the Peace Convention to Congress on February 27, 1861. This made it clear that those who controlled the South would not voluntarily return to the Union on terms acceptable to Republicans who controlled the central government.[18] Nor would many northern Democrats accept the terms of the South.

None of the prominent Democrats in Indiana, such as Congressman Daniel Voorhees and Thomas A. Hendricks, went so far from what was politically possible as Milligan. This was the situation when Milligan associated with others who opposed the Civil War for many reasons, some honorable and some dishonorable. This confused Milligan's issue of constitutionality. The most important of those with whom Milligan associated was Harrison H. Dodd. He was not careful to stay within the law and when tested proved to be a runaway.[19]

It is not difficult to understand why a military commission decided that Milligan should be hanged. Rather, it is difficult to understand why, except for the trial by a military commission, Milligan never seemed to be in any personal danger, never had to prove himself in personal encounters as Vallandigham did.

The *Democrat* associated Milligan with the men who drafted and ratified the Constitution: "We cannot believe it was ever the intention of the framers of the Constitution, that it should be held together by force. That patriotism and fraternal love were the ligaments by which they hoped to hold together, and when these fail, and when all efforts to compromise the difficulties are exhausted, the only policy to be pursued is the peaceable separation of the opposing elements and a treaty of amity between them as independent nations."[20]

Such a separation was not considered permanent. The "people South must be relieved of this notion of subjugation. They will never be compelled to do what they even desire to do. They will resist to the last man, woman and child. This is now the lever by which the revolutionists move their States and keep down opposition. Let the people see that they come back by their own free will and on honorable terms, and they will come. The people South love the great republic. It is a slander upon their taste and judgement to say that they do not. Give them but a chance and this glorious Union will be preserved; and in no part of the country will the event be hailed with more heartfelt exultation than in the South."[21]

The invective of Milligan was aimed at the sources of moral authority for those who used killing and destruction to preserve the Union. One of these sources was enthusiasm for the flag. Milligan asserted that he would rather "spit upon the stars and stripes than to see them at the head of an army marching forth in the present crisis."[22] Another source was religion. Milligan asserted that he had "no faith in the final restoration of the Union . . . no prayers to offer in behalf of the soldiers, or for the cause in which they are engaged."[23]

Three sources of authority for those who supported the Union were Governor Morton, President Lincoln, and army officers. Concerning Morton, Milligan asserted that Morton's proclamations were "silly twaddle."[24] Concerning Lincoln, Milligan asserted that the war was "unjust, unnecessary, infamous,"[25] that he did not hate the rebels of the South nearly as much as the Lincoln administration.[26] Milligan had only contempt for army officers and referred to them as "shoulder straps."

Those who supported Milligan commended such statements.[27] Those who opposed him considered them proof that he was a traitor.[28]

However, friends of Milligan sounded a warning note from their memories of Aaron Burr: After Burr had been tried for treason, he attempted to resume the practice of law; but he was lightly esteemed by his fellow citizens and died in poverty.[29] That Milligan was successful in protecting himself from such a fate is

Change Resisted by Milligan

evident from the fact that he quickly reestablished himself in law practice after the war.

In July 1861 the Democrats in Huntington County had a meeting to establish unity. This resulted in so much hostility that James R. Slack gave a slight wound with a penknife to John R. Coffroth.[30] This did not presage the result of the next encounter when Milligan took the initiative.

Slack and Milligan met at the Democratic county convention on August 10, 1861. Slack advanced the interpretation that the war was caused by the treasonable conduct of citizens of the rebellious states and must be suppressed. Milligan denounced Slack for sacrificing principle for political expediency. Slack was silenced.[31] Indeed all of the War Democrats were silenced in Huntington County.

Milligan, chariman of the committee of resolutions, worked on the reasoning that was later perfected in the Fort Wayne Speech. The fifth resolution declared that the keeping up of the army lately so wickedly and unconstitutionally raised, and under the command of abolitionists and unscrupulous adventurers, was inconsistent with the liberties of the people, and already presented the frightful proportions of military despotism.

The sixth resolution declared that "We have no sympathy with the cause of Secession, and do not believe that in the election of Abraham Lincoln to the Presidency, Abolitionist and Sectionalist as he was known to be, the Confederate States had any just cause to withdraw from the Union. But the fact is too apparent . . . That neither written Constitutions, nor official oaths afford any guarantee against the licentiousness of the administration, and that in the wanton and palpable violations of the Constitution of the United States, in the suspension of the writ of *habeas corpus,* in depriving citizens of liberty and property without due process of law; in the levying of war by the President; in raising an army; in providing and maintaining a navy; in giving preference to commerce to the ports of one State over another; in the unreasonable search and seizure of persons and papers; in the desecration of houses and homes of citizens; in the subjection of the press; in the prostitution of the telegraph; in the abridgement of the liberty of speech and like wrongs and usurpations, we have witnessed the overthrow of constitutional liberty in America."

The eighth resolution declared that while disapproving of the war in which the soldiers were engaged, there was confidence in their gallantry and courage. They "have our kindliest wishes for their welfare, and safe and speedy return to their friends and their homes."[32]

The first election after the beginning of the war was in October 1861. Election of the Union candidate for county commissioner, the only contest, was interpreted by the Democrats to have resulted from the defection of the Slack faction.[33]

Quite different was the outlook for the Republicans. An increasing demand for cereals improved the prospects for farmers and businessmen. The editor of the *Herald* "wears a saintly smile, now; his step is more elastic, and he seems buoyed up, generally, by the flattering prospects ahead of the 'good time coming.' "[34]

Compromise proposals by the Democrats gave way to war news. There was assurance that the government would take good care of the Huntington boys. Claims were made that the Democrat party was the only party with enough vigor to prosecute the war and reconstruct the Union, that the Democrat party had been Lincoln's reliance from the day the war began, that the Democrat party could restore the Union with the help of loyal sentiment in the South when it was positively shown that this was not an abolition war.[35]

In December Milligan, as chairman for the Huntington County central committee, invited Democrats to a meeting to select representatives for the state convention: "Not for a moment could we entertain the idea that a platform would be there arranged inimical to the Government, or the Administration, if it deviates not from a performance of its legitimate functions. We cannot well conceive how so absurd a notion, as that the Democracy sympathizes with rebellion, could have obtained currency. Is it not notoriously true, that nearly two-thirds of the army are Democrats, and these, certainly, will not be accused of sympathy with rebellion? Is it not equally true that Democrats, in civil pursuits, everywhere, have

Change Resisted by Milligan 51

given the most unequivocal manifestations favorable to a prosecution of the war, inside of the Constitution?"[36]

A surge of war spirit and their own confusion had weakened the Democrats in 1861. Reaction to the burdens of war helped them in 1862.[37] Both in Cincinnati and Indianapolis it was noticed that the resolutions of the Democratic people in Huntington County "are ably drawn and speak in no undecided or delphic tone. As their spirit and character are likely to be adopted in the West, they are worth a careful perusal."[38]

However, the thinking of the Democrats in Huntington County on arbitrary arrests and emancipation was uneven. No arbitrary arrests "should have ever been made, and could not, if justice and law had not been set aside. Every arrest was but an act of persecution for opinion's sake, and the blackest page in American history, will be that upon which is recorded the acts of the President in regard to the political arrests."[39]

Emancipation with compensation was opposed because "Even if the North could afford to pay the additional tax to free the negro, we apprehend there are but few who would favor the consummation of the project. The inevitable consequence of emancipation would be that the North (the negro's ideal of the land of 'milk and honey,' a counterpart of the 'happy land of Canaan,') would be flooded with the worthless, thieving colored population, who would settle down as permanent inhabitants; and, competing with our white laborers, would reduce their wages, and by contact degrade them."[40]

In January 1862 Milligan participated in the state convention. The ninth and tenth resolutions were commended by the *Democrat* as conservative, worthy of the approbation of every Democrat and every loyal citizen. The ninth stated "that this war should not be waged in a spirit of conquest or subjugation, not for the purpose of overthrowing or interfering with the rights or institutions of the States, but to defend and maintain the supremacy of the Constitution, and to preserve the Union with all the dignity, equality and rights of the several states unimpaired; and that as soon as these objects are accomplished the war ought to cease." The tenth stated "That we will sustain with all our energies a war for the maintenance of the Constitution, and of the integrity of the Union under the Constitution; but we are opposed to a war for the emancipation of the negroes, or the subjugation of the Southern States."[41]

Those considered by the *Democrat* worthy to be Congressmen would sustain General George B. McClellan and others who were waging war for the Constitution. On this basis Milligan was recommended to be a candidate.[42]

The *Democrat* recognized that Milligan was not personally popular, but considered this "as 'dust in the balance' when weighed with his ability and patriotism."[43] However, the Democrat party was more sensitive to what was politically expedient and nominated James F. McDowell for the Eleventh District. The *Democrat* supported McDowell.

On September 20, 1862, at the Huntington County Fair Grounds, using a farm wagon as a speaker's platform, Milligan introduced Thomas A. Hendricks as Indiana's favorite son. The Democrats were elated at the size of the crowd which they estimated to be over two thousand.[44]

Although a severe critic of Lincoln's administration, Hendricks was keenly aware of what was politically advantageous. He had been president of the Democrat state convention in January. There he had opposed national emancipation on the basis that slavery was a state question, opposed the tariff because it would raise the prices of manufacturd goods, and gave as the proper aim of the war the restoration of the Union under the Constitution.[45]

Throughout Indiana in 1862 there was a swing from support of the Union party in June to the Democrat party in October. Economic measures of Lincoln's administration had resulted in national debt, resort to paper money, large land grants and loans to private corporations, and the raising of the tariff. There had been arbitrary arrests, interference of the military with civilian affairs, violation of freedom of speech and the press, and the suspension of the writ of habeas corpus for persons charged with disloyal practices. Failure to win the war was very disappointing. Reassertion of abolition raised the question of the purpose of the war and the sincerity of earlier statements by President Lincoln that the war was to preserve the Union.[46]

In October the entire Democrat ticket was elected in Huntington County.[47] This was interpreted by Milligan as a triumph of constitutional liberty over usurpation and despotism. His explanation was that "the great conservative element . . . only require to know the right to do it." He urged the Democrats not to "relax our efforts, but organize, not in the fabulous order of the Knights of the Golden Circle, or any other secret legion, but in clubs in every township, and hold regular and public meetings for the discussion of the issues involved in the present crisis, and for the raising of means for the purchase and distribution of documents and papers and encouraging a more general circulation of Democratic Journals among the people, to the end that the delusion cast over the nation by twenty years' labor of false priests and demagogues may be dispelled, and the right of truth felt and realized throughout the land; then will your arm be strong—then will your rights be secure."[48]

In the course of 1862 news about and speeches of Clement L. Vallandigham of Ohio were published in the *Democrat*. Considerable attention was also given to Governor Horatio Seymour of New York. Both of these men interpreted the victory of the Democrats in 1862 to mean that the people wanted the war speedily terminated. Both held forth the hope that reconciliation with the South was possible if fair and honorable means were used. Seymour took the position that "our armies in the field must be supported —all constitutional demands of our General Government must be promptly responded to . . . Under no circumstances can the division of the Union be conceded."[49] Vallandigham relied less on force. In his letter dated July 15, 1863, accepting the Democrat nomination to be governor of Ohio, he noted that all of those in the South with whom he had talked were determined not to surrender. But "when the war shall have ceased and invading armies been withdrawn" they were ready "to consider and discuss the question of reunion. And who shall doubt the issue of the argument?"[50]

Before the year (1862) ended, the Democrats in Huntington

County were involved in a miscalculation that was politically disastrous. They concurred in the erroneous estimation of the situation which considered that the Union could never be restored by force of arms.

At the Huntington County Democrat Convention on December 6, 1862, it was resolved that "had it not been for the fanaticism and peculation of New England, our generation would not have witnessed the ghastly specter of disunion, and were it not for the same cause still potent for evil, those difficulties could readily be adjusted." Consequently, should New England continue to stand in the way of restoration of the Union as it was and thus prevent the Western men from uniting with others in the Mississippi Valley, "Then will we cheerfully say to New England, with all her cupidity, with all her meanness, fanaticism, follies, and moral turpitude, we bid you good bye, remembering you only for the wrongs you have done us."[51]

Further arguments for a Northwestern Confederacy were that, when dependent upon markets in the East, railroads would charge what they pleased and the high protective tariff would enrich the Eastern States. It was asserted that free navigation of the Mississippi River and free trade were best for the Northwest.[52]

These arguments were based on the conviction that the majority of the American people assumed at the time of the ratification of the Constitution state withdrawal was possible if the Union should prove unsatisfactory.[53] One prominent man who furthered separation was Congressman William J. Allen from Illinois. He was arrested in 1862 for openly advocating that Illinois be divided and the southern part join the Confederacy. Because of "old associations" President Lincoln in September 1862 urged Allen's discharge. Lincoln even considered that Congressman Allen would be a good man to support the Union.[54]

The folly of a Northwestern Confederacy was soon recognized and quickly abandoned by the *Democrat*. But army officers did not forget. They interpreted it as the work of conspirators who continued to aid the South.[55] For practical army officers any man who opposed the war was a traitor. Since Milligan opposed the war with vigor and ability, it was only a question of time until he would be arrested. It made no difference that "we take pride in rendering a cordial support to our Government in the exercise of all its constitutional functions, without stopping to question their propriety, save at the hustings and ballot-box...."[56]

NOTES

1. Lloyd Lewis, *Myths After Lincoln* (New York, 1929), p. 405.
2. Jack Lindeman, ed., *The Conflict of Convictions* (New York, 1968), p. 211.
3. William B. Hesseltine, *The Tragic Conflict: The Civil War and Reconstruction* (New York, 1962), p. 18.
4. Benjamin P. Thomas and Harold M. Hyman, *Stanton: The Life and Times of Lincoln's Secretary of War* (New York, 1962), p. 116; A. K. McClure, *Lincoln and Men of War Times* (Philadelphia, 1962), p. 260.
5. Wood Gray, *The Hidden Civil War: The Story of the Copperheads* (New York, 1942), p. 141.
6. Robert H. Abzug, "The Copperheads: Historical Approaches to Civil War Dissent in the Midwest," *Indiana Magazine of History* (March 1970), LXVI:40-55.
7. Huntington, Indiana, *Herald,* December 22, 1899.
8. Huntington, Indiana, *Democrat,* December 30, 1863.
9. Frank L. Klement, *The Copperheads of the Middle West* (Chicago, 1960), p. 267.
10. Roscoe Pound, "Constitutional Guarantees of Liberty," *Nebraska Law Review* (1945-1946), XXIV-XXV:60.
11. James Willard Hurst, *Law and the Conditions of Freedom in the Nineteenth Century United States* (Madison, 1956), pp. 24, 32.
12. *Democrat,* November 8, 1860; Ray Ade, *History of the Democratic Party in Huntington County* (Huntington County Historical Society, 1957), p. 3.
13. John D. Barnhart and Donald F. Carmony, *Indiana: From Frontier to Industrial Commonwealth,* 4 vols. (New York, 1954), II:157.
14. *Democrat,* January 10, 1861.
15. *Herald,* December 15, 1899; Florence L. Grayston, "Lambdin P. Milligan: A Knight of the Golden Circle," *Indiana Magazine of History* (1947), XLIII:391.
16. James L. Vallandigham, *A Life of Clement L. Vallandigham* (Baltimore, 1872), p. 160.

17. *Herald,* February 20, 1861.
18. James G. Randall and David Donald, *The Divided Union* (Boston, 1961), p. 242.
19. Some friends of Milligan believed that Dodd was a spy for Governor Morton and that the assignment of Dodd was to get Milligan to violate law and thus become subject to punishment as well as to be discredited, that Dodd was permitted (even helped) to escape in order to further in the public mind that Milligan and others were guilty. *Democrat,* June 7, 1866. See footnote 68 in Chapter VIII.
20. *Democrat,* June 1, 1861.
21. Ibid., July 4, 1861; Clement Eaton, *The Waning of the Old South, Civilization, 1860-1880's* (Athens, 1968).
22. *Herald,* June 5, 1861; DeLong commented: "Those who instigated the meeting, at such an untimely period in our country's history, will die the death of traitors and rebels, and their memories be overwhelmed in everlasting infamy."
23. Ibid., July 8, 1863.
24. Ibid., July 30, 1862.
25. *Democrat,* October 2, 1862.
26. *Herald,* September 16, 1863.
27. *Democrat,* August 12, 1863.
28. *Herald,* June 5, 1861.
29. *Democrat,* August 1, 1861.
30. Ibid., July 25, 1861; ibid., August 1, 1861.
31. Ibid., August 15, 1861. Note Chapter IV, quotation for footnote 35.
32. Ibid., August 15, 1861.
33. Ibid., October 17, 1861.
34. Ibid., October 31, 1861.
35. Ibid., November 14, 1861; ibid., November 28, 1861.
36. Ibid., December 5, 1861.
37. Olin Dee Morrison, *Indiana at Civil War Times* (Athens, 1961), p. 126.
38. Quoted from the Cincinnati, Ohio, *Enquirer* in the Indianapolis, Indiana, *Daily State Sentinel,* December 25, 1862.
39. *Democrat,* February 27, 1862.
40. Ibid., March 27, 1862.
41. Ibid., January 16, 1862.
42. Ibid., March 27, 1862.
43. Ibid., August 14, 1862.
44. Ibid., September 25, 1862.
45. Ibid., January 23, 1862. In 1863 Hendricks was elected to the United States Senate. In 1872 he was the first Democrat to be

Change Resisted by Milligan

elected governor of Indiana after the Civil War.
46. Barnhart and Carmony, *Indiana: From Frontier to Industrial Commonwealth,* II:168-170.
47. *Democrat,* October 16, 1862.
48. Ibid., October 23, 1862.
49. Ibid., January 22, 1863.
50. Vallandigham, *A Life of Clement L. Vallandigham,* p. 321.
51. *Democrat,* December 18, 1862. In the *Democrat,* March 27, 1862, the Northwestern Confederacy was favored "unless the Union can be restored as it was, with all her institutions unimpaired."
52. Ibid., January 15, 1863; ibid., January 29, 1863.
53. James G. Randall, *Constitutional Problems Under Lincoln* (Urbana, 1951), p. 16.
54. Roy Basler, ed., *The Collected Works of Abraham Lincoln,* 9 vols. (New Brunswick, 1953-1955), V:427.
55. W. H. H. Terrell, *Indiana in the War of the Rebellion: Report of the Adjutant General* (Indianapolis, 1960), p. 384.
56. *Democrat,* December 18, 1862. This was one of the resolutions adopted December 6, 1862. Milligan probably drafted all of the resolutions. One resolution, only offered, has his name: "That we are in favor of a commerce based on the principles of free-trade; a revenue upon an equitable system of direct taxation, a currency composed of gold and silver only."

Chapter VII

Triumph of Lincoln, 1863-1864

By the beginning of 1863 President Lincoln had accepted the main changes necessary to preserve the Union. By the end of 1864 he had achieved decisive military victory and political affirmation. Nevertheless, this was accompanied by developments that made Lincoln more vulnerable to some points in the legal position of Milligan.

President Lincoln did what was necessary to preserve the Union without resorting to extremism. But he had no way to prevent the spread of the idea that the Constitution was in abeyance during the war. Others, with little regard for law, did what each considered "necessary." Army officers, Congress, governors, businessmen, and writers found this a convenient principle.

The result was increasing confusion. Men lost confidence in others following the law. Since often force, not law, was the decisive factor, individuals and organizations prepared to use force.

President Lincoln never ceased fighting the legalism of Milligan that would have permitted a state to leave the Union. But, as this was deprived of practical significance, Lincoln became more concerned with using what was intended by those who drafted the Constitution to place limits on Congress, economic interests, and the military. Relationship with Congress was least involved in Milligan's fight against Lincoln. Relationship with economic interests was not vital. Relationship with the military enabled Milligan to win partial victory.

On December 1, 1862, President Lincoln made a well-reasoned call to accept change: "The dogmas of the quiet past are inadequate to the stormy present. The occasion is piled high with

Triumph of Lincoln

difficulty, and we must rise with the occasion. As our case is new, so we must think anew and act anew."[1]

Although contrary to what was desired by Lincoln, one problem of the "stormy present" was disregard for law by merchants in the northeastern ports.[2] What preserving the Union was for Lincoln, profit was for some businessmen. Profit was secured by trading with the enemy.

After the Civil War the problem of law in connection with economic interests was more important than the problem in connection with the military. But for President Lincoln the military was more demanding. He was as firmly opposed to extreme military thinking as he was to states leaving the Union. Consequently, he noted on January 26, 1863, when he placed Major General Joseph Hooker at the head of the Army of the Potomac "your recently saying that both the Army and the Government needed a Dictator. Of course it was not for this, but in spite of it, that I have given you the command."[3]

Probably the best statement of military thinking was made by Ulysses S. Grant after his career as general and president of the United States. His thinking was strengthened by being considered in accord with that of Lincoln's secretary of war, Edwin Stanton: "The Constitution was not framed with a view to any such rebellion as that of 1861-1865. While it did not authorize rebellion it made no provision against it. Yet the right to resist or suppress rebellion is as inherent as the right of self-defense, and as natural as the right of an individual to preserve his life when in jeopardy. The Constitution was therefore in abeyance for the time being, so far as it in any way affected the progress and termination of the war."

Furthermore, "Those in rebellion against the government of the United States were not restricted by constitutional provisions, or any other, except the acts of their Congress, which was loyal and devoted to the cause for which the South was then fighting. It would be a hard case when one-third of a nation, united in rebellion against the national authority, is entirely untrammeled, that the other two-thirds, in their efforts to maintain the Union intact, should be restrained by a Constitution prepared by our ancestors for the express purpose of insuring the permanency of the confederation of the States."[4]

During the Civil War, it would have been to Lincoln's advantage to have been able to rely on civil courts. Nearly all cases had been tried before civil courts during the Amrican Revolution and the writ of habeas corpus was available.[5] Contemporaries of Lincoln were accustomed to civil courts.

But Lincoln became convinced that judges interpreted the law in a way that provided aid for the overthrow of the government.[6] After he had appointed judges, he still did not rely upon them.

Lincoln's alternative to civil courts, military arrests with trials by military commissions, also presented difficulties. It was not easy to draw a line to indicate where military officers should and should not use this method. Some 13,535 men were arrested and confined in military prisons from February 1863 to the end of the war. Usually they were held in prison without a trial and released when no longer considered dangerous. The justification was that "The arrests in all cases were of men who had been detected in treasonable correspondence with rebels, or whose sympathy with the rebellion and defiance of the Government were notorious."[7]

The best-known man arrested before Milligan was Vallandigham. Although President Lincoln commented that "in my own discretion, I do not know whether I would have ordered the arrest of Mr. Vallandigham," he defended the arrest, trial, and conviction on the ground that there had been desertion and resistance to the draft due more to Vallandigham than any other man.[8]

Democrats, meeting at Albany to protest the arrest of Vallandigham, promised to support President Lincoln in every constitutional and lawful way to suppress the rebellion. This placed him in a position to reply: "I have not knowingly employed, nor shall knowingly employ, any other. But the meeting, by their resolutions, assert and argue, that certain military arrests, and proceedings following them for which I am ultimately responsible, are unconstitutional. I think they are not. . . . By the third resolution the meeting indicates their opinion that military arrests may be constitutional in localities where rebellion actually exists; but that such arrests are unconstitutional in localities where rebellion, or insurrection does not actually exist . . . . Inasmuch, however, as the constitution itself makes no such distinction, I am unable to think that there is any such constitutional distinction."[9]

Lincoln observed that the rights of citizens were secured after civil war in England, and after the American Revolution: "I, too, am devotedly for them after civil war, and before civil war, and at all times 'except when, in cases of Rebellion or Invasion the public Safety may require' their suppression . . . . Of how little value the constitutional provisions I have quoted will be rendered, if arrests never shall be made until defined crimes have been committed, may be illustrated by a few notable examples." These examples were of men high in the Confederacy who could have been arrested to keep them from providing leadership for the South. Thus, "Nor am I able to appreciate the danger . . . that the American people will, by means of military arrests during the rebellion, lose the right of public discussion, the liberty of speech and the press, the law of evidence, trial by jury and Habeas Corpus, throughout the indefinite peaceful future, which I trust lies before them . . . ."[10]

Nevertheless, Lincoln realized that he might be wrong and gave the reason: "If I be wrong on this question of constitutional power, my error lies in believing that certain proceedings are constitutional when, in cases of rebellion or Invasion, the public Safety requires them . . . ."[11]

It was this question that made Lincoln vulnerable to the legal attack by Milligan. There were Republican as well as Democrat judges who had little confidence in future Presidents of the United States.

More concerned with immediate problems, in 1863 DeLong hoped that Milligan, or at least those associated with him, would recognize that Lincoln's reasoning "bears in its plainness of language, directness of thought and frankness of purpose, the unerring marks of its distinguished author, while the aptness and force of its arguments are equal to the best of his writings. It is a paper which should be carefully considered by all citizens, and especially by those liable to be led by political associations and prejudice into opposition to the wise policy here so well defended."[12]

Closely associated with Milligan was J. R. Coffroth, who ceased to be in opposition to "the wise policy." Both Milligan and DeLong, as well as others, requested Coffroth to publish his address, delivered on July 4. After much flowery rhetoric Coffroth reached the point: "The Constitution must be maintained: the Union must be preserved, and our flag must be upheld."[13]

In the same issue that contained the address by Coffroth, DeLong reported that after a parade of eighty to one hundred mounted men, Milligan made a speech "exceedingly inflammatory ... heartily endorsed by a few of the ignorant rabble who surround him, and are ever willing to do his bidding." In other words, Milligan did not follow Coffroth in changing.

But President Lincoln's reasoning was persuasive: "As the war progresses ... the necessity for arbitrary dealing ... gradually decreases. I have every reason to desire that it would cease altogether . . . ."[14] In accord with this, "thoroughly imbued with a reverence for the guaranteed rights of individuals, I was slow to adopt the strong measures, which by degree I have been forced to regard as being within the exceptions of the constitution, and as indispensable to the public safety . . . . Civil courts are organized chiefly for trials of individuals, or, at most, a few individuals acting in concert; and this in quiet times, and on charges of crime well defined in the law."[15]

Caution about "strong measures" was a portent for how far Lincoln would go in his opposition to Milligan. In September 1862 and again in September 1863 Lincoln suspended the writ of habeas corpus in cases of military arrest, but the suspension was only for "the duration of the said rebellion . . . ."[16]

In September 1863 his attorney general, Edward Bates, expressed the opinion that there was "a general and growing tendency of the military, wherever stationed, to engross all power."[17] In October 1863 Lincoln's instructions to General John M. Schofield were that "There is no organized military force in avowed opposition to the general government, now in Missouri . . . you will only arrest individuals, and suppress assemblies, or newspapers, when they may be working palpable injury to the Military in your charge; and in no other case will you interfere with the expressions

Triumph of Lincoln

of opinion in any form, or allow it to be interfered with violently by others."[18]

As Lincoln stated on April 4, 1864, "I felt that measures, otherwise unconstitutional, might become lawful, by becoming indispensable to the constitution, through the preservation of the nation. Right or wrong, I assumed this ground, and now avow it."[19] Increasingly self-restrained, when suspending the writ of habeas corpus in Kentucky on July 5, 1864, he concluded that "The martial law . . . will not be deemed or taken to interfere . . . with the administration of justice in the courts of law existing therein between citizens of the United States in suits or proceedings which do not affect the military operations or the constituted authorities of the Government of the United States."[20]

A little more than a month earlier Lincoln had accepted renomination. A little more than a month later he gave a cue to army officers and political supporters: "The weal or woe of this great nation will be decided in the approaching canvas. My own experience has proven to me, that there is no program intended by the democratic party but that will result in the dismemberment of the Union."[21]

He had many reasons to be depressed in August 1864. The credit of the government was low. His administration was opposed not only by the Peace Democrats but also by Radical Republicans. The military situation was characterized by nonaction and reverses. In his opinion the Democrats would probably be successful in the approaching election.[22] His attention turned to Indiana because "The State election of Indiana occurs on the 11th of October, and the loss of it to the friends of the Government would go far toward losing the whole Union cause."[23]

One of the proposals based on this conclusion was not fully approved. Governor Morton wanted to defer the draft and return fifteen thousand soldiers to Indiana before the election in order to vote. However, President Lincoln was only willing to further the return of sick and wounded soldiers.

Within Indiana Morton was unrestrained by Lincoln. With his usual vigor Morton set forth at length the well-known allegation that the Democrats were traitors: The Sons of Liberty, a secret organization of Democrats, were conspiring for a Northwestern Insurrection (also called Northwestern Conspiracy). Accusations were followed by military arrests.

There had been so many cases of military arrests that Lincoln paid little attention to the accusations and military arrests in Indiana. What was unusual in Indiana, and this prompted immediate response from Lincoln, was that one of the men arrested was John B. Castleman. He had been a captain in the Confederate army under the command of General John H. Morgan.

Castleman went to Chicago at the time the Democrats had their national convention to nominate a candidate for president of the United States. He was accused of having plans to assist the Sons of Liberty in a Northwestern Insurrection.

Lincoln drafted an order for the commanding officer, Major General Alvin P. Hovey: "Whenever John B. Castleman shall be tried, if convicted and sentenced, suspend execution until further order from me, and send me the record."[24]

This order was not sent to General Hovey but was entrusted with Judge Samuel M. Breckinridge of Missouri whose wife was a sister of John Castleman. Lincoln did this for "Sam" and his wife, and the order was not to be made public unless there was an emergency. Actually the order was never used because Castleman was released without trial on condition that he leave the United States.

President Lincoln's practicality and humaneness had a strong appeal when presented in Huntington County by DeLong: The only sure way to preserve the Union was for patriotic men to fulfill their obligation to defend the country by defeating the Secessionists; this was the way to stand with Washington, Jefferson, and Jackson.[25]

A quotation from Washington in 1775 was used to confirm this: "As it is now very apparent that we have nothing to depend upon in the present contest but our own strength, care, firmness, and union, should not the same measures be adopted in your and every other government on the continent? Would it not be prudent to seize on those tories who have been, are, and that we know will be, active against us? Why should persons who are preying on the vitals of their country be suffered to sulk at large, whilst we know they will do us every mischief in their power?"[26]

Although not so appropriate for DeLong, Jefferson recognized that on great occasions every good officer must be ready to risk himself by going beyond the strict line of the law.[27] Jackson was outspoken against rebels and traitors.[28]

DeLong quoted from a book that had been published in 1862, *The Trial of the Constitution by Sidney G. Fisher*. Especially noted was the position of George Washington when some twenty men had been arrested in Philadelphia at the insistence of Congress: "They were not treated as criminals, but with consideration and kindness. Those who chose to declare their allegiance to the Government were released, and all were permitted to return to their homes when it was thought they could no longer be dangerous. These arrests were made with the knowledge and approbation of Washington. A writ of *habeas corpus* was issued at the insistence of the prisoners, but it was disregarded by the officer in charge of them, and soon afterwards, September 16th, 1777, the Legislature passed a bill indemnifying the Executive Council, and suspending the writ of *habeas corpus*."[29]

As significant as the part of Fisher quoted by DeLong was the part omitted: "The great principles of the Constitution are true. The machinery by which they were meant to be carried out is for the most part well contrived for the purpose. But its defects must be corrected." To do this "The powers of Congress must . . . be unlimited, if they are to be 'adequate to the exigencies of the Union' . . . . This power is nothing more than the latent and reserved, but absolute and despotic authority, which every government must possess, to use in case of need. If it be not granted by the Constitution, it must be employed nevertheless, for we cannot resort to the process of the Fifth Article. If the Union and the Government cannot be saved out of this terrible shock of war constitutionally, *a* Union and *a* Government must be saved unconstitutionally."[30] The part of Fisher omitted was as much in opposition to President Lincoln as military arrests without *habeas corpus* were to Milligan.

A liitle material for DeLong was supplied by Colonel Slack of the 47th Regiment. He was a capable combat officer with a keen sense of what was practical. In February 1863, when in Arkansas, he signed a statement that unjustified opposition to the war was giving aid and comfort to the enemy, that the South was leaning on the Northern Democracy for support.[31] Colonel Slack had combat duties. But his point of view was ably expressed in Indiana by Governor Morton. As much as any combat officer, he was the incarnation of will to win the war.

After the Democrats won control of the state legislature in 1862, Governor Morton went further than President Lincoln in exercising power on the basis of war necessity. Governor Morton had few scruples about military arrests. He raised and dispersed money without the authority of law for two years.[32]

DeLong was in accord with much that was done by Governor Morton.[33] But when the governor sent arms to various parts of the state, DeLong took a defensive position: None were needed in Huntington County as loyal men were already well supplied with arms and ammunition.[34] Nor was DeLong favorably impressed by the work of Henry B. Carrington who was working for Governor Morton.[35] However, DeLong accepted military arrests, denounced opposition to the war as disloyal, and considered that Democrats controlled the state legislature only because sixty thousand loyal men were out of the state.[36]

When victory for the Union party in the local election in October 1863 revealed a trend away from the Democrats, DeLong had scathing remarks: "The so-called Democratic party, by the semi-treasonable and suicidal policy into which it has been forced by Southern emissaries and unscrupulous Northern demagogues in the loyal States, made as fatal a mistake as did the tories in the Revolution, and the Federalists in the War of 1812; and its leaders will very soon discover, if they have not already discovered, that no party can be popular which opposes the national cause and gives aid and comfort to the enemy in a time of war—especially a civil war, like that the country is now afflicted with. The people are patriotic, and will repudiate any party or politician that is not so."[37]

Nevertheless, prospects for the Republicans were far from

Triumph of Lincoln

good. Only Democrats had been reelected to the presidency by any political party, Washington being reelected before parties were organized. No Democrat had been reelected after President Andrew Jackson. During the summer of 1864 General Grant seemed to accomplish nothing, war casualties were an increasingly heavy burden, the Republican party was split over war aims and reconstruction, the financial position of the government was weaker, and there were more calls for troops.[38]

DeLong recognized that the Union as it was could not be restored. Nor did he want it entirely restored. The Union as it was had included slavery and DeLong believed that slavery perverted the first principle of human freedom on which the country was based. He also rejected state loyalty before loyalty to the country. His "Union as it is to be" would have "one political faith, one Union, one glorious destiny."[39]

As the election approached in 1864, DeLong was in a difficult position. What was being charged against the Democrats and what he knew to be true in Huntington County were too far apart.

Governor Morton had authorized the publication of an exposition of an organization called the Sons of Liberty. The allegations were: it was a secret treasonable organization; Clement L. Vallandigham was the Supreme Commander for the United States; Harrison H. Dodd was the Grand Commander for Indiana; Indiana was divided into four military districts; each of these had a major general; Milligan was listed as one.[40]

There was no question about Democrats preparing for the next election campaign. The question concerned the strength, control, and purpose of the Sons of Liberty. According to the exposition, the alarming purpose was to assassinate Governor Morton and other high officials, separate the Northwestern states from the Union, and either form a separate government or become a part of the rebel confederacy.[41]

This was in the summer of 1864 before the victories in September. Military men who were not only obeying the orders of General Grant but also were in accord with his thinking reasoned thus: (1) Troops needed to fight General Robert E. Lee were required in the Northern states to prevent Southern prisoners from being released; (2) there were dangerous men in the North who, if they had leadership and the opportunity that might come from some success of the South, would weaken the North by burning northern cities, by poisoning water supplies, by spreading disease, and by blowing up river and lake steamers; (3) the Northern press was "free up to the point of open treason"; part of it was eager to magnify Southern success and to belittle the success of the Union army; (4) the North would be "much stronger" with a hundred thousand of those who opposed the Lincoln administration in the Confederate ranks and the rest "thoroughly subdued" as the Union sentiment was in the South.[42]

A gulf developed between military thinking and that of De Long: "We are not ready to believe that the masses of the people of Indiana, calling themselves Democrats, are ready to follow desperate conspirators, like Dodd, into civil war, that would desolate the State, and bring universal mourning into the households to its inhabitants."[43] No mention was made of Milligan in connection with Dodd.

Early in September there was the good news that General William T. Sherman had occupied Atlanta, Georgia. Later in the month came the good news of the "Great Victory" of General Philip Henry Sheridan.

Military thinking that called for thoroughly subduing those who opposed the Lincoln administration was unacceptable to De Long after the first victory: "Heated discussions result in no good . . . every man has a perfect right to talk of and vote for whom he pleases."[44]

DeLong went further after the second victory: "Five thousand peace Democrats were arbitrarily arrested on the 19th inst., in the Shenandoah Valley, by a wild Irishman named Sheridan. We do not remember to have heard of a more flagrant violation of the Constitution since the formation of the Government."[45] Another news story retracted so far as to call Sheridan a "most thorough and accomplished soldier."[46]

It was generally recognized that the victories of Sherman and Sheridan would probably secure the reelection of Lincoln. The election in Indiana was also influenced by the trial of Harrison

Triumph of Lincoln

H. Dodd. Because of his association with Dodd and others, Milligan was implicated. He was arrested on the morning of October 5, 1864, at his home. The order for his arrest was issued by General Alvin P. Hovey, commanding the district of Indiana.

The *Personal Memoirs* of U.S. Grant contain numerous references to Hovey which present him as a capable combat officer. What Hovey did in regard to Milligan was in accord with the thinking of Grant although he was not directly involved in the move to silence Milligan.[47] Of course, as President Lincoln had stated in connection with the arrest of Vallandigham, Lincoln was "ultimately responsible."

NOTES

1. Huntington, Indiana, *Herald,* December 10, 1862.
2. Ludwell H. Johnson, "Commerce Between Northeastern Ports and the Confederacy, 1861-1865," *Journal of American History* (1967), LIV:34.
3. Roy Basler, ed., *The Collected Works of Abraham Lincoln,* 9 vols. (New Brunswick, 1953-1955), VI:63.
4. Ibid., VI:78; U.S. Grant, *Personal Memoirs,* 2 vols. (1885-1886), II:506-507.
5. Bradley Chapin, "Colonial and Revolutionary Origins of the American Law of Treason," *William and Mary Quarterly* (1960, XVII:16.
6. Basler, *Works of Lincoln,* V:285.
7. W. H. H. Terrell, *Indiana in the War of the Rebellion: Report of the Adjutant General* (Indianapolis, 1960), p. 305. Reprint of Volume I of the eight volumes published in 1869. James G. Randall, *Lincoln: The Liberal Statesman* (New York, 1947), p. 126; Basler, *Works of Lincoln,* V:436-437.
8. Basler, *Works of Lincoln,* VI:269.
9. Ibid., VI:262, 265; *Herald,* June 24, 1863.
10. Basler, *Works of Lincoln,* VI:262-267.
11. Ibid., VI:267.
12. *Herald,* June 24, 1863.
13. *Herald,* July 15, 1863. See also reference to Coffroth in Chapter VIII.
14. Basler, *Works of Lincoln,* VI:269.
15. Ibid., VI:264.

16. Basler, *Works of Lincoln,* V:436; VI:451.
17. Quoted from Bates to J. G. Knapp, September 16, 1863, in Marvin R. Cain, *Lincoln's Attorney General: Edward Bates of Missouri* (Columbia, 1965), p. 267.
18. Basler, *Works of Lincoln,* VI:492.
19. Ibid., VII:281.
20. Ibid., VII:426.
21. Ibid., VII:506.
22. Albert Mordell, comp., *Selected Essays by Gideon Welles: Lincoln's Administration* (New York, 1960), p. 180.
23. Basler, *Works of Lincoln,* VIII:11. Lincoln observed that Indiana was the only important state voting in October whose soldiers could not vote in the field.
24. Ibid., VIII:123.
25. W. Lewis Roberts, "The Citizen's Obligation Under the Constitution," *Kentucky Law Journal* (1955-1956), XLIV:170; Allan Nevins, *The Statesmanship of the Civil War* (New York, 1953), p. 13; Carl Russell Fish, *The American Civil War* (New York, 1937), p. 1.
26. *Herald,* January 14, 1863.
27. Ibid., February 4, 1863.
28. Recent historians confirm that Jefferson, too, was not always adverse to suppressing opponents. Leonard W. Levy, *Legacy of Suppression: Freedom of Speech and Press in Early America* (Cambridge, 1960), p. 301.
29. *Herald,* March 4, 1863.
30. Sidney George Fisher, *The Trial of the Constitution* (Philadelphia, 1862), pp. 55, 199.
31. *Herald,* February 18, 1863. This was also signed by Brigadier General Alvin P. Hovey (who was later important for Milligan) and three other colonels.
32. Morton's defense can be found in his "Speech to Answer Joseph E. McDonald," dated July 28, 1964, *Morton Papers,* Archives Division, Indiana State Library.
33. *Herald,* January 21, 1863.
34. Ibid., January 4, 1863.
35. Frank L. Clement, "Carrington and the Golden Circle Legend in Indiana during the Civil War," *Indiana Magazine of History* (1965), LXI: 52.
36. *Herald,* February 4, 1863.
37. Ibid., October 21, 1863.
38. James G. Randall and David Donald, *The Divided Union* (Boston, 1961), pp. 454, 473.
39. *Herald,* February 10, 1864.

40. Ibid., August 3, 1864.
41. Terrell, *War of the Rebellion,* p. 383.
42. Grant, *Personal Memoirs,* II:502.
43. *Herald,* August 24, 1864.
44. Ibid., September 14, 1864. This issue included the letter of acceptance of McClellan, which the *Herald* called a "fraud and a deception," and a letter of General Grant on the crisis—"a straight-forward paper."
45. Ibid., September 28, 1864.
46. Ibid., October 5, 1864.
47. Grant, *Personal Memoirs,* I: 519 et passim.

Chapter VIII

Milligan Antagonizing Precedents, 1863-1864

Milligan emerged in 1863-1864 because his legalism gave him power. Unfortunately for him, few who cheered his invective at political rallies shared this legalism.[1]

During 1863 and 1864 the Democrat who continued to be best known nationally for his opposition to the war was Clement L. Vallandigham of Ohio. In Indiana the Democrats best known for opposition to the war were Thomas A. Hendricks and Daniel W. Voorhees.

Vallandigham, in a speech that was eight columns long when published in the *Democrat,* insisted that it was possible to end the war. He reasoned that since the Union was consent, goodwill, and fraternal affection, the solution was to "Stop fighting. Make an armistice—no formal treaty. Withdraw your armies from the seceded states . . . ," reestablish economic and social relations, let slavery alone, and choose a new president in 1864.[2]

Some Republicans believed that unless the war was ended by negotiation Democrats were sure to win the next election.[3] Voorhees strove to make this prophecy come true: "Neither indemnity for the past nor impunity for the future can be bestowed on those who have violated, and who propose further to violate, the great and fundamental principles of constitutional liberty." Specifically, "If the American people—deceived, betrayed, and outraged—are unwilling to support the war policy of this administration any longer, unless coerced to do so by such legislation as this conscription bill, then let us stop fighting at once, and try what virtues there may be in peaceful remedies."[4]

The *Democrat* prepared a six-column review of the policies of Lincoln in the form of a trial.[5] The case against Lincoln assumed that when the invading army no longer possessed the soil, the ballot box would do its work and the South would return to the Union under a Democrat administration.[6] Lincoln was accused of destroying the states and establishing consolidated despotism: No state had been able to protect its citizens and their property; martial law had been proclaimed in every state; the writ of habeas corpus had been suspended; the bank bill took from the states the regulation of banking; and the military bill placed all ablebodied men under the president instead of calling on the states for a quota.[7]

Not only Lincoln but also Jefferson Davis confounded those who proposed to rely on the ballot box. The decisions of Jefferson Davis, president of the Confederacy, were based on what he stated in July 1864: "As these proposals had been prefaced by the remark that the people of the North were a majority, and that a majority ought to govern, the offer was, in effect, a proposal that the Confederate States should surrender. . . ."[8]

Instead of peaceful remedies, the use of force increased in the North. At the time of the military arrest of Vallandigham on May 5, 1863, the *Democrat* asserted that "Since the outbreak of the rebellion, the scullions of abolitionism have dogged his footsteps, and caught up his utterances in the hopes of contorting them into treason as defined by abolitionism. Mr. Vallandigham knows his rights and privileges under the Constitution and we have not the remotest idea that he will take one step beyond. It can scarcely be doubted that he was arrested under the late order forbidding the free discussion of the 'war policy' of the Administration, which is no crime. Free discussion is guaranteed by the Constitution and it shall be upheld though the whole country must pass through the ordeal of another revolution."[9] The late order referred to was that of Brigadier General Milo S. Hascall. Suppression of newspapers and arrests were justified in part of point two of his General Orders No. 9: the "country will have to be saved or lost during the time that this Administration remains in power."[10]

In May 1863 Thomas Hendricks was driven from the platform in Indianapolis by soldiers and vilified as a butternut.[11] In December Daniel W. Voorhees sent to Governor Oliver P. Morton an extract cut out of a newspaper which reported the governor to have said: "I warn those in the North who are understood (or supposed) to sympathize with the rebellion, or with traitors, 'to flee from the wrath to come.' When the war was successfully over that class would be outlawed, their homes would be made desolate and their wives and children would become outcasts."

Then Voorhees added: "It is true that I know of no party in the North whose members sympathize with treason or rebellion, save perhaps the extreme abolition wing of your party. I therefore would appropriate none of your threat to me or mine if you had not yourself already given it an application. You have often charged that the Democratic party was in sympathy with the doctrines by which it is maintained. The entire press of your party has clamored with similar accusations. By you then, the Democratic party is 'understood or supposed to sympathize with the rebellion or with traitors.' This understanding and this supposition on your part I know to be false; but it shows unerringly toward whom you aimed the atrocious threat which I enclose, if you gave utterance to it at all. These two sentences attributed to you, simply, in your view of politics, propose to outlaw one hundred and thirty thousand Democrats in Indiana, desolate their homes, and make outcasts of their wives and children."[12]

A more immediate difficulty was that the Democrat party searched unsuccessfully for a constructive program. A majority of the Democrats in a district meeting at Fort Wayne weakly proposed no armistice, nor withdrawal of armies, or cessation of hostilities until the South would ask for negotiation.[13] Neither the district resolutions nor those made at the state convention which met on May 20, 1863, contained a program that seriously challenged the Lincoln administration.

Milligan was in the minority on the committee at Fort Wayne that drafted resolutions. He thought that the majority had much intelligence and moral worth, but did not comprehend the Constitution as expounded by Jefferson.[14]

Milligan was further isolated by a move toward furthering goodwill between Democrats and Republicans in Huntington County. J. R. Coffroth delivered the speech for the Fourth of

Milligan Antagonizing Precedents

July celebration in 1863. This was probably the only local speech during the Civil War that was published in full in both the *Democrat* and the *Herald*.

Milligan refused to participate in the meeting.[15] He was antagonistic to the spirit of accommodation shown by Coffroth that proclaimed "the Constitution, the Union, and the flag, are the essentials of the patriot's faith, and in that there should be unity; the means of their preservation is a non-essential tenet, and in it, therefore, there should be allowed liberality of opinion; and in both there should be charity."[16]

This speech was being prepared for publication in the newspapers when on July 8, 1863, General John H. Morgan invaded southern Indiana. A rumor quickly spread that those who opposed the Lincoln administration were responsible for Morgan determining upon this course. Democrats were confronted with "the anxious disposition felt in every locality to assist in catching and chastising the invaders."[17]

Bending to Coffroth, the *Democrat* attempted to resolve difficulties: "The true policy of those who are in favor of suppressing the rebellion, but opposed to abolitionism, is to rally to the old Democratic standard and strive to keep it free from errors of secession and abolitionism, and pledged to the vigorous prosecution of the Constitution, to restore the Union, and to the constitutional settlement of its consequences."[18]

With such a feeble basis Coffroth tried to rally the Democrats for the election in October. He spoke for "the Union as it was, and the Constitution as it is." He spoke against the confiscation and emancipation measures of the Lincoln administration.[19] The result was that the Democrats lost the local election.[20] This was part of a wider loss. Lincoln had reason to rejoice because Pennsylvania, Ohio, and Indiana were "all right."[21]

With the Democrat party losing to the Republicans, and Milligan losing out in the Democrat party, he had occasion to be encouraged by his true source of strength in legal confrontation with those acting under the authority of President Lincoln.

Alexander J. Douglas, a state senator from Columbia City, Indiana, about twenty miles north of the home of Milligan, was arrested on May 13, 1863, in Ohio. His trial was before a military commission in Cincinnati, Ohio. Milligan was a counsel for Douglas.

The *Democrat* "recalled that this trial took place immediately after the trial of Mr. Vallandigham and in the height of the military despotism that reigned over the district of Ohio under the Fredricksburg butcher; and the coolness and neatness with which Mr. Milligan successfully justified the whole conduct of the accused is but another evidence of that master mind which most of our readers have had other opportunities of appreciating."

Moreover, "We can imagine we see that hidden leer of contempt for shoulder-straps as well as for the recent decision of Judge Leavitt in the following double entendre: 'He had equal confidence in the legal capacity of the members of this Court, and their judicial integrity with the Court to which it should have been legally referred,' for what could have been more ridiculous than a set of shoulder-straps sitting in judgment on the right of free speech, unless it was the decision of Judge Leavitt in denying the writ of *habeas corpus* in the Vallandigham case."[22]

The charge against Douglas was that he had violated General Order No. 38. On May 29, 1863, before pleading, Milligan stated that "The defendant moves the Court to dismiss this case, because the Court has no jurisdiction of the person of the defendant nor the subject-matter of the charge; in this, that the specifications do not show that the defendant was in the military service, either land or naval. Nor does said specification state facts sufficient to constitute any offense of which this Court has Jurisdiction." This motion was declined by the military commission.[23]

Mlligan then presented the plea of not guilty: Vallandigham had been the advertised speaker at the meeting, but was arrested; Douglas made an extemporaneous speech to people who were excited because the arrest seemed so full of danger; the Sedition Act of 1798 allowed the truth of words to be given in evidence; the truth was that there were two political parties, one friendly to the administration and one distrustful; to accuse Democrats of being traitors gave aid and comfort to the enemy; the statements

Milligan Antagonizing Precedents

of Douglas did not, as charged, show that he favored the enemy or resisted laws.

Douglas, stated Milligan, "recognizes no Government as ours whose powers are not founded on the constitution of the United States, the principles of which are rendered more sacred and glorious by the perils to which its votaries are daily exposed. . . . I cannot but believe that this arrest is the result of a misconception on the part of the witnesses of the facts and legal import of the case, and that the prosecution would never have been instituted had the department been advised of the facts in the case and, therefore, ask that the defendant be discharged."[24]

These ideas and much of this language had been hardened and polished by lawyers and judges in cases involving arbitrary arrests before Milligan defended Douglas. The chief spokesman for the Democrats in Indiana who furthered these legal principles was Judge Samuel E. Perkins who was on the Indiana Supreme Court.[25] But it was to be Milligan who combined time, place, opportunity, and tenacity to fight through to victory in the Supreme Court of the United States.

Parts of the basis on which Milligan made his stand appeared from time to time in the *Democrat*. Early in 1864, using five columns, the development of the United States was traced through the Declaration of Independence, the treaty with Great Britain, the Articles of Confederation, the Constitution of the United States, the constitutions of Indiana, and the administrations of Jefferson and Madison: "It is not a question of argument, but of fact, that the American people are not a Nation, but a Confederation, or a Confederate Republic, composed of the United States. These United States elect the President and Senate, and the President and Senate create the Supreme Court, make treaties with foreign powers, appoint the Federal or Confederate functionaries. In short, constitute the government; while the House of Representatives, intended certainly to represent the whole people, may aid in voting to carry on the government, but possess no intrinsic or special power of any kind whatsoever."[26]

The relationship between these problems and politics in

Indiana was that if Democrats secured control of the state in the next election many of the acts of Governor Morton would probably be condemned as unconstitutional. If Republicans secured control, the whole matter would probably be dropped or laws passed approving what he had done.[27]

How remote Milligan was from what was politically possible can be seen by a statement of Congressman Voorhees. He warned the Southern people "not to look forward to separation and independence, but to embrace every opportunity for cooperation with the conservative men of the North, who will aid with their lives, if need be, to secure them all their rights and institutions as free and equal citizens of the United States. If this be done, the approaching presidential election will bring peace, union, and liberty."[28]

Nearly all Northern Democrats were in accord with the practical political position of Voorhees, not the legalism of Milligan, as voting later revealed. However, Southern Democrats rejected the suggestion of Voorhees. Moreover, Milligan, secret organizations of the Democrats, and illusions of a Northwestern Confederacy got confounded as convenient targets for campaign material of Republicans.[29]

DeLong accepted the Republican targets up to a certain point. A secret organization of Democrats, commonly called Knights, was often referred to and names of members in Huntington County were published. But, instead of being dangerous, the Knights were considered cowardly, miserable men who sneaked to sterile meetings. The Knights were not supposed, by DeLong, to be able to stand up even to their opponents in the Democrat party. Milligan was not listed among the Knights.

Such were the prospects when Milligan, with his usual disregard for political possibilities, considered being a candidate for governor. If nominated by the Democrats, and elected, he would be governor when the constitutionality of what Governor Morton had done was reviewed. Also Milligan would be in a good position to oppose President Lincoln on state rights.

Democrats who controlled the state organization would not support Milligan because they wanted a candidate who had the most favorable prospects for a political victory. But there was a Democrat, Harrison H. Dodd, who desired to further the political aspirations of Milligan.

The letter that Milligan wrote to Dodd on May 9, 1864, is the only letter written by Milligan that is available. Milligan's commitment was clear: "As to the Gubernatorial question, it may not have occurred to you the unenviable connection in which my name has been used. It was announced in consequence of the declination of Hon. J. E. McDonald to be a candidate, conceding that if he was a candidate there was no desire to use my name; now I understand he is; hence I am not called upon by any public notice to be such. But waving all this as a result of mere accident, and not proffered as an indignity to me, by placing me second in talents and patriotism to J. E. McDonald, there is still a more grave difficulty in the way. The announcement of my name for Governor, was made by McDonald's friends. Now it is due to them that I should decline, because I could not represent them; there is no similarity between us. And all this is not so discouraging as the fact that men of the stamp of Judge Hanna, whose profession of principles I could represent, prefer McDonald on account of his supposed availability, it detracts much from my confidence in our ultimate success. When men of so much seeming patriotism are willing for mere temporary purposes to abandon the great principles of civil liberty, what will those of less pretensions do, when the real contest comes, when life and property all depend on the issue, when bullets instead of ballots are cast, and when the haltar is a preamble to our platform? For unless Federal encroachments are arrested in the States by the effort as well of the legislators as the executive, then will our lives and fortunes follow where our honors will have gone before."[30]

Nevertheless, Milligan continued to be a candidate: "I can conceive of no emergency that can justify Federal encroachments" on the sovereignty of a state, "and hold it to be the most sacred duty of the State Executive to exert whatever force may be necessary to protect the people of his State against all unlawful intrusions upon their peace and liberty, and expel from the State all agents of usurpation and tyranny."

Moreover, "Fully convinced that the war is without sanction in morals or the theory of our government . . . I shall leave no effort unmade to terminate the effusion of blood at the earliest period possible, believing, as I do, that the restoration of peace without a separation of the agricultural States of the Union is the only means by which the people of Indiana can be saved from the absolute and irreparable subjugation from a system of class legislation, exactions and oppression dictated alone by Puritanic rapacity. For he is not gifted in political analogisms who cannot see in the history of the anti-Democratic party for the last half century the most unmistakable evidence of a purpose on their part to reduce the people of the West to a state of pecuniary vassalage to the commercial and manufacturing interests of the East."[31]

Milligan's statements were greeted by Republicans with derision. What he needed was a schoolmaster not the office of governor. He got his ideas from the old Confederation instead of the Constitution. His inordinate vanity enabled political tricksters to get him to be a candidate. Few Democrats would support him. Milligan's statements were rank with treason and the hallucination of state sovereignty. They promised a degree of physical courage which those who had seen him tried could scarcely believe he possessed.[32]

The prediction concerning support for Milligan was as canny as the sneer about courage was wrongheaded. Widespread success of the Democrats in 1862 had shown that the party was capable of victory. In spite of Republican gains in 1863, prospects were good for the Democrats in 1864. Decline of morals, high taxes, loss of life in battle, control of Mexico by France, violations of civil liberties, profiteering, and inroads on state rights weakened the Union party.[33]

Most Democrat leaders in Indiana considered it fortunate that Vallandigham had been defeated in his campaign in 1863 to be governor of Ohio.[34] They were opposed to Milligan because he was less practical than Vallandigham. Consequently, when Milligan's name was presented to be a candidate for governor he was overwhelmingly defeated by Joseph E. McDonald.[35]

As was clear in his letter to Dodd, Milligan was motivated by his opposition to the legal precedents being established by President Lincoln. Such a position almost separated him from practical Democrat politics. The state platform pledged to support the war to preserve the Union. It went no further to include the position of Milligan than to charge that the actions of the Republicans were revolutionary and subversive of the Constitution of the United States.[36]

Thus Milligan got practically nothing from being a candidate for governor. He lost much. Association with Dodd occasioned Milligan's nadir. Dodd aroused suspicion as Grand Commander of the Knights in Indiana. He was vulnerable to the accusation of getting money from the Confederates in Canada. It took the influence of J. J. Bingham, chairman of the Democratic State Committee, to get Dodd to abandon schemes of an armed uprising. Dodd was arrested and Milligan was implicated.

After his failure to be a candidate for governor, Milligan completed the preparation of his legal challenge to President Lincoln. Milligan had an opportunity to present this in his Fort Wayne speech on August 13, 1864.[37] Even the editor of the *Democrat* considered this speech "not suited to the occasion" and "not calculated to create any enthusiasm among the masses."[38] Democrat newspapers in Fort Wayne ignored Milligan's speech and Republican newspapers made the usual use of the invective to discredit all Democrats.

As practical Democrats knew, the military situation made Milligan's legalism of no importance for the war. As analyzed in the report of Lieutenant General Grant: "On the night of the 2nd of July, Sherman commenced moving his army by the right flank, and on the morning of the 3rd, found the enemy, in consequence of this movement, had abandoned Kenesaw and retreated across the Chattahoochee. General Sherman remained on the Chattahoochee to give his men rest and get up stores until the 17th of July, when he resumed his operations, crossed the Chattahoochee, destroyed a large portion of the railroad to Augusta, and drove the enemy back to Atlanta. At this place General Hood succeeded General Johnston in command of the rebel army, and assuming the offensive-defensive policy, made several severe attacks upon

Sherman in the vicinity of Atlanta, the most desperate and determined of which was the 22nd of July. . . . In all these attacks the enemy was repulsed with great loss . . . on the 2nd of September [Sherman] occupied Atlanta, the objective point of his campaign."[39]

However, to the editor of the *Democrat,* the Fort Wayne speech was "a logical and unanswerable refutation of the fallacy that a war against a State can be constitutionally waged."[40] Neither President Lincoln nor any of his apologists refuted what Milligan considered should control interpretation of the Constitution: The use of force against a state was not intended by those who drafted and ratified the Constitution.

How far Democrats who controlled the party were from Milligan's thinking was indicated by the rumor that they wanted General Grant to be their candidate for President.[41] Actually they nominated General George B. McClellan.

Circumstances at the time McClellan was nominated, and later Northern victories, destroyed his chances to be elected. Vallandigham, the candidate preferred by the *Democrat,* had been able to get some of his ideas in the platform. McClellan repudiated these ideas and called for prosecution of the war on the basis that no peace could be permanent without the Union. Accepting practical politics, Vallandigham supported McClellan. After Atlanta fell on September 2, 1864, and the North rallied for final victory, President Lincoln was in a strong political position.[42] With this development the best political argument for the Democrats would have been to prosecute the war more vigorously.[43]

Milligan, who had been a delegate to the National Convention, was the first to speak at the local meeting in Huntington after McClellan was nominated. Milligan was not satisfied with the nomination and would vote for McClellan only if the letter of acceptance were satisfactory. Thereupon, Coffroth raked Milligan "fore and aft" for "throwing a wet blanket on the ardor of the faithful."[44]

It was worse for Milligan personally. He had been overwhelmingly rejected by the Democrat party in Indiana. He was out of sympathy with those who controlled the national organization. He was opposed by a friend, Coffroth, locally. Then, suddenly, when placed under arrest on October 5, 1864, he was catapulted from the field of politics where he was ineffective to the field of law where he was strong.

By this time military arrests split both the Democrats and the Republicans. As DeLong pointed out such arrests had been made by order of McClellan when he was General in Chief of the Army.[45] President Lincoln supported army officers in military arrests but had written to Major General Ambrose E. Burnside at the time of the arrest of Vallandigham: "All the cabinet regretted the necessity of arresting . . . Vallandigham, some perhaps, doubting that there was a real necessity for it—but, being done, all were for seeing you through with it."[46]

Governor Morton thought military arrests strengthened Democrat opposition to the war. He urged that if military rule were needed for the Northwest, the state government aided by the federal government should handle such problems.[47]

With this reasoning he continued the discussion begun about four months earlier. Governor Morton was having much trouble carrying out his plans to support the war because Democrats controlled the state legislature. He sent a letter to President Lincoln summarizing the program of the Peace Democrats: to end the war by whatever means, to recognize the Confederacy, and to propose a reunion leaving out the New England states. Governor Morton also described the secret Democrat societies which he believed intended to sabotage the Union. He requested Lincoln to meet him at Harrisburg.

Lincoln gave his answer on February 1, 1863: "I think it would not do for me to meet you at Harrisburg. It would be known, and would be misconstrued a thousand ways. Of course if the whole truth could be told and accepted as the truth, it would do no harm, but that is impossible."[48]

In spite of what Governor Morton had recommended, the department commanders continued to control military arrests. In the detailed report of the secretary of war that specified measures for national defense there was no mention of a military problem in the Northwest.[49] However, after the raid on October 19, 1864, by a band of Confederates who crossed the Canadian border into Vermont, President Lincoln mentioned "inimical and desperate persons" in Canada.[50]

By the time Milligan was arrested there had been so many arrests that everything connected with them was well worked out.[51] Consequently, there was little unusual about Milligan's arrest, trial by a military commission, or the opposition to the trial except Milligan's conviction that he was legally right and that to compromise this right was worse than being hanged.[51]

On the basis that the North should win the war, military commissions were justified.[52] The purpose was to silence those who made it more difficult to win. Almost any indication that a man would accept being silenced brought release. Escape was easy. When there was a trial and sentence, in every case before Milligan some way to eliminate the effectiveness of the man and grant a pardon or suspend the sentence had been found.

Democrats at the time of Milligan's arrest[53] and scholars since[54] have amply considered the arrest from the standpoint of the election. Beyond question Governor Morton wanted to win. For a short time after the arrest of Milligan the local Democrats were demoralized. Nevertheless, to arrest, try, and punish Milligan was primarily a military decision. The evidence for this is the reasoning of the judge advocate at the trial.

The military commission used methods that had been perfected during centuries of use. A group was accused of conspiracy. If, for any reason accepted by the army officers on the commission, one was guilty, everyone considered by them to be in the group was guilty and could be sentenced to death.

The reaction of Coffroth was not to question the necessity of placing Milligan under arrest but to try to get the case before a civil court.[55] The reaction of DeLong was that the "testimony in the Dodd case went far in establishing the fact that Milligan had some connection with Dodd and others in a conspiracy to overthrow the Government and inaugurate civil war in this and other Northern states. If, upon thorough investigation, it is found that Mr. Milligan has been guilty of crime, he should be properly punished. If he is innocent, an investigation of his conduct can do no harm."[56] DeLong denied that any Republican in Huntington had anything to do with Milligan's arrest and "it is useless to say they can exert any influence in securing his return."[57] DeLong also denied a desire to see the editor of the *Democrat* or any of his friends arrested, and claimed to have "invariably protested against it when we had an opportunity for so doing."[58]

The next day after the arrest of Milligan, J. J. Bingham, Democrat editor of the Indianapolis *Daily State Sentinel,* was arrested. In an editorial on October 3, 1864, he had charged that the trial of Dodd was gotten up for partisan purposes to win the elections. Furthermore, "The trial of Mr. Dodd before a military commission is a mockery. Indiana adheres to the Federal Government. Never has there been a time when the mandates of her courts could not be enforced by the civil authorities."[59]

Three aspects of the situation helped Milligan. The proceedings of the military commission were made available;[60] the military commission kept him where he could press for a trial in a civil court; and the thinking of some of the judges in the lower courts was favorable.[61] Had Milligan been sent to the Confederacy, as was done in Kentucky to silence Lieutenant Governor Richard T. Jacobs about this same time, President Lincoln could have given the same answer: "You are at liberty to proceed to Kentucky, and to remain at large as far as relates to any cause now past. In what I now do, I decide nothing as to the right or wrong of your arrest, but act in the hope that there is less liability to misunderstanding among Union men now than there was at the time of the arrest."[62]

In Indiana, as in Kentucky, military men had good reason to be determined that certain speakers should be silenced. The Confederates were face to face with defeat and used money to bribe men in the North. Prisons crowded with captive Confederate soldiers were not well guarded and some of the prisoners still wanted to fight. Some men in the North, presumably Democrats, used violence against military officers. There was a political organization among the Democrats organized along military lines.[63] In the event that the South had an important victory or secured the alliance of another nation, there was the possibility that the northwestern states would have a general uprising, form a separate government, and might even join the Confederacy.[64]

Although when General John H. Morgan invaded Indiana he had secured only opposition from Democrats who had been accused of aiding the South,[65] in July and August 1864 (the darkest hour of the conflict)[66] the military commission before which Milligan appeared was convinced of the danger of an uprising.

Facts that convinced the military mind were counteracted by other considerations. Although both Republicans and Democrats had organizations that used military titles, and Milligan's name had been placed on paper as a major-general, he never held the office.[67] H. S. Zumro, a medical doctor in Markle, was a spy who tried without success to trap Milligan. Dodd had implicated Milligan, yet had easily escaped. The *Democrat* thought Dodd was a "tool and fellow conspirator" with Governor Morton who was trying to find "a pretext to massacre in cold blood the Democratic masses."[68]

Unrestrained by such considerations, the military commission proceeded according to the Proclamation of President Lincoln dated September 24, 1862. This made liable, during the insurrection, to trial and punishment by military commission all guilty of disloyal practices which offered aid and comfort to the enemy.[69]

Although often done at the time, and since, there is no reason to impugn the motives of those involved. A contemporary statement about the high quality of the Supreme Court[70] should also be applied to Governor Morton, the military commission, and Milligan as well as Lincoln.

The principle on which Governor Morton made his decision was right: President Lincoln needed governors who supported the war. The principle on which the military commission made its decision was right: In war the will to win must come first. The principle on which Milligan made his decision was right: The precedent to not follow the intent of those who drafted and ratified the Constitution tended to destroy the rule of law. The principle on which President Lincoln made his decision was right: Without the Union there was neither the political nor the economic strength to preserve liberty. In short, there was a constitutional crisis.[71]

Milligan Antagonizing Precedents

The trial at Indianapolis was sensational. Those arraigned with Milligan were Dodd, W. A. Bowles, Andrew Humphreys, H. Heffren, and Stephen Horsey. What made Milligan quite different from the others was that he absolutely refused to compromise in order to keep from being hanged. Especially in connection with Milligan caution must be used to approach "accurate, thoroughly documented, and impeccable history."[72]

Men on the military commission were nearly all colonels in the infantry, Indiana Volunteers. They followed the principle stated by Judge Advocate Major H. L. Burnett: "The civil rights of the citizen become dead for the time being, if necessary to preserve the life of the nation."[73] At the time, a consciousness that the North was wrong would have caused defeat;[74] unwillingness to pay the price of victory would have caused defeat.[75] Since these were two main points in Milligan's Fort Wayne speech, his civil rights were dead so far as the military commission was concerned. They were determined to silence him, by hanging if no other way was found. He was troublesome because he stood firm and fought.

Milligan was physically sick at the time of his arrest and during much of the time in prison. But he was not bothered by any psychological problems. He believed that God favored his cause. He identified with those dedicated to law. He had intense pride and unshakable confidence in the inherent right of his thought and action. He had no doubt about release if the Supreme Court heard his case.[76]

From the standpoint of winning the war, the military commission did valuable work.[77] Nevertheless, certain developments prepared the way for Milligan to gain the advantage. The spies who provided information for the military commission were men whose reputations for telling the truth was poor. They got much of their information by leading men on to treasonable action and then betraying confidence. The evidence of military preparation to establish that there was a great dangerous conspiracy was not convincing.[78] DeLong accepted that Dodd was a desperate conspirator, but did not believe that the mass of Democrats would follow him into Civil War and desolate the state.[79] Lincoln did not believe that 160,000 Democrats in Indiana were disloyal.[80]

It was only on the basis of a conspiracy in the opinion of a military commission, in which everyone who was considered to have any connection was guilty, that Milligan was in danger from the charges against him. In one address in defense of Milligan, John R. Coffroth pointed out that by the common law of practice there was nearly always granted a separate trial for persons jointly charged with felony.[81] However, a separate trial was refused by Judge Advocate H. L. Burnett: Conspiracy was the gist of the charge and proof against one was proof against all. Therefore, "we may prove against Milligan the acts of Dodd, and the testimony introduced by Milligan that he did not do these acts himself, constitutes no defense for him. When he takes upon himself the responsibility of joining an unlawful body, he takes upon himself the responsibility for every unlawful act of that body."[82]

As counsel for Milligan pointed out, this ruling made liable to the death penalty thousands of Democrats who were assumed to have joined either the Knights or the Sons of Liberty. Both Republican and Democrat civilians were concerned.[83] DeLong observed that "Mr. John Roche was before the Military Commission at Indianapolis last week, and testifies to the good moral character and loyal reputation of Mr. Milligan. Mr. Roche stated that Milligan was not now nor never had been a member of a secret political organization. We are glad to hear this latter statement."[84] Six months later, DeLong went further; "We do not now, nor never did, indiscriminately endorse the conduct of military commissions, especially in States not in rebellion, and where the civil courts are in unrestrained operation."[85]

Coffroth's defense of Milligan before the military commission took the position that Milligan was a loyal man who expressed extreme political views. So far as Dodd was concerned, Milligan had no knowledge of his schemes until after they had been abandoned. There was no evidence for any of the inculpatory circumstances charged against Milligan. Referring to the fourteen years he and Milligan had practiced at the same bar, Coffroth stated: "With his extreme political views I have held no sympathy —for the Sons of Liberty I have had no respect; but I will never believe that Mr. Milligan, either in act or heart, is a traitor."[86]

From Roche and D. O. Dailey, a lawyer from Huntington who was not sympathetic with Milligan, the military commission heard the most penetrating statements about Milligan. Roche: "I have heard Mr. Milligan make remarks, in which he held that some of the officers of the Government were exceeding their authority, and he complained that they were not acting according to law."[87] Dailey: "As a lawyer I think him very able; as a politician I do not think he amounts to anything at all, for this reason, he takes special occasion to publish the most ultra and obnoxious sentiments. . . ."[88]

However, considering Milligan from the military standpoint, the judge advocate singled him out for the harshest condemnation: he was "the right arm of this conspiracy in this State; the active, energetic, and venomous leader. A man of unquestioned ability and determination, and with a heart full of hatred, envy, and malice, he moved forward in this scheme of revolution with a coolness and intensity of purpose, not exceeded by any other member of the conspiracy."[89]

The decision was to hang Milligan. It was a decision that some on the military commission reached reluctantly and accepted because it seemed likely Lincoln would find another way as he had done in each previous case.[90]

Milligan was sent first to the Soldier's Home at Indianapolis and later to the Ohio Penitentiary. DeLong commented that Milligan was hard at work on more honorable business than when at home.[91] Those who favored Milligan only agreed that the treatment was hard.[92]

Although Governor Morton had a majority over McDonald in Huntington County soon after the arrest of Milligan, McClellan had a majority over Lincoln. This caused DeLong to lament that "Our country, we regret to say, is already in rather bad odor wherever known, and such results tend rather to increase than diminish the load of odium."[93]

The "load of odium" was political. That Milligan's legalism so far as the war was concerned had been annihilated did not escape President Lincoln: "No candidate for any office whatever, high or low, has ventured to seek votes on the avowal that he was for giving up the Union. . . . In affording the people the fair opportunity of showing, one to another and to the world, this firmness and unanimity of purpose, the election has been of vast value to the national cause."[94]

NOTES

1. Those who opposed the war had heterogenous sources for their ideological commitments. Richard O. Curry, "The Union As It Was: A Critique of Recent Interpretations of the Copperheads," *Civil War History* (March, 1967), XIII: 39.
2. Huntington, Indiana, *Democrat,* February 5, 1863.
3. Ibid., February 12, 1863.
4. From speeches dated February 18 and February 23, 1863. Charles S. Voorhees, ed., *Speeches of Daniel W. Voorhees of Indiana* (Cincinnati, 1875), p. 126.
5. *Democrat,* March 26, 1863; April 16, 1863; July 30, 1863; August 27, 1863.
6. Ibid., March 5, 1863.
7. Ibid., March 19, 1863.
8. Jefferson Davis, *The Rise and Fall of the Confederate Government,* 2 vols. (New York, 1881), II:611.
9. *Democrat,* May 7, 1863.
10. Ibid., April 30, 1863.
11. Bartness to wife, May 21, 1863, Smith Library, Indianapolis.
12. Daniel W. Voorhees to O. P. Morton, December 11, 1863, Foulke Collection, Indiana Division, State Library and Historical Building, Indianapolis.
13. *Democrat,* May 7, 1863.
14. Ibid., May 14, 1863.
15. Huntington, Indiana, *Herald,* July 8, 1863. See reference to Coffroth in Chapter VII.
16. *Herald,* July 15, 1863; *Democrat,* July 16, 1863.
17. W. H. H. Terrell, *Indiana in the War of the Rebellion: Report of the Adjutant General* (Indianapolis, 1960), pp. 211, 224.
18. *Democrat,* September 10, 1863.
19. Ibid., October 8, 1863.
20. Ibid., October 15, 1863.
21. Roy Basler, ed., *The Collected Works of Abraham Lincoln,* 9 vols. (New Brunswick, 1953-1955), VI: 515.
22. *Democrat,* August 6, 1863.
23. Ibid.

Milligan Antagonizing Precedents

24. Ibid.
25. Emma Lou Thornbrough, "Judge Perkins, the Indiana Supreme Court, and the Civil War," *Indiana Magazine of History* (1960), LX: 80, 95.
26. *Democrat,* January 7, 1864.
27. Indianapolis *Daily State Sentinel,* January 19, 1864.
28. C. S. Voorhees, ed., *Speeches of D. W. Voorhees,* p. 173. Speech in the House of Representatives, March 5, 1864.
29. *Herald,* March 16, 1864.
30. Benn Pitman, ed., *The Trials for Treason at Indianapolis, 1864* (Cincinnati, 1865), pp. 88-89.
31. *Daily State Sentinel,* July 8, 1864; Fort Wayne, Indiana, *Daily Times,* June 21, 1864; *Democrat,* June 30, 1864.
32. *Herald,* July 6, 1864.
33. *Democrat,* June 16, 1864; W. Birkbeck Wood and James E. Edmonds, *Military History of the Civil War* (New York, 1937), p. 307; William Frank Zornow, *Lincoln and the Party Divided* (Norman, 1954), p. 6.
34. Emma Lou Thornbrough, *Indiana in the Civil War Era 1850-1880* (Indianapolis, 1965), p. 211.
35. *Democrat,* July 14, 1864.
36. Ibid., July 14, 1864; *Herald,* July 20, 1864.
37. Darwin Kelley, ed., "Lambdin P. Milligan's Appeal for States' Rights and Constitutional Liberty during the Civil War," *Indiana Magazine of History* (1970), LXVI:263. This included the entire speech.
38. Benn Pitman, ed., *The Trials for Treason at Indianapolis, 1864* (Cincinnati, 1865), p. 173.
39. U. S. Grant, *Personal Memoirs,* 2 vols. (New York, 1885-1886), II:588-589.
40. *Democrat,* August 18, 1864.
41. *Herald,* March 9, 1864.
42. Ibid., September 14, 1864.
43. Hugh McCulloch, *Men and Measures of Half a Century* (New York, 1888), p. 162.
44. *Herald,* September 7, 1864.
45. Ibid.; *Report and Evidence of the Committee on Arbitrary Arrests in the State of Indiana* (Indianapolis, 1863).
46. Basler, *Works of Lincoln,* VI: 237.
47. Ibid.
48. Ibid., 87-88. This is the only reference in these volumes to the Northwest Confederacy.
49. Thirty-eighth Congress, 2nd Session, 1864-1865, House Executive Document, No. 83 (Washington, 1865).

50. Basler, *Works of Lincoln*, VIII:141.
51. Jacob Mogelever, *The Story of Lafayette C. Baker, Lincoln's Secret Service Chief* (New York, 1960), p. 416.
52. James G. Randall, *Lincoln, The Liberal Statesman* (New York, 1947), p. 132; James G. Randall, *Constitutional Problems Under Lincoln* (New York, 1926), p. 521.
53. *Democrat*, October 13, 1864.
54. Kenneth M. Stampp, "The Milligan Case and the Election of 1864 in Indiana," *Mississippi Valley Historical Review* (1944), XXXI: 43; Patrick W. Riddleberger, *George Washington Julian, Radical Republican: A Study in Nineteenth Century Politics and Reform* (Indianapolis, 1966), p. 200.
55. *Democrat*, October 13, 1864.
56. *Herald*, October 12, 1864.
57. Ibid., October 26, 1864.
58. Ibid., November 2, 1864.
59. *Daily State Sentinel*, October 3, 1864.
60. Basler, *Works of Lincoln*, VIII: 190. This refers to the opinion of the attorney general on January 3, 1865, concerning naval court-martial.
61. Thomas McIntyre Cooley, *A Treatise on the Constitutional Limitations which Rest Upon the Legislative Power of the States of the American Union* (Boston, 1890), p. 222.
62. Basler, *Works of Lincoln*, VIII:182, 222.
63. Document No. 83. *Military Operations in Indiana, 1864-1865, Report of Brevet Major-General Alvin P. Hovey*, Archives Division, Indiana State Library.
64. Terrell, *War of the Rebellion*, p. 384.
65. James Ford Rhodes, *History of the United States from the Compromise of 1850*, 7 vols. (New York, 1904), V:317.
66. J. G. Randall and Richard N. Current, *Lincoln the President: Last Full Measure* (New York, 1955), p. 156; Horace Greeley, *The American Conflict*, 2 vols. (Hartford, 1867), p. 664.
67. This point was later confirmed in the Indianapolis *Journal*, May 22, 1871.
68. *Democrat*, November 10, 1864. Dodd later returned to the United States and again entered politics. No effort was made to punish him. A letter to me from Dick Sprague, a descendant of Dodd, indicates that Dodd could not have been a spy. This letter is in the Indiana Division of the State Library. Considering the later political decisions of Dodd, it seems probable that he had worthy motives; but was not frank with associates, was deficient in the ability to make plans, and was not careful to follow law. At the time of his arrest, in Dodd's office were found four hun-

dred revolvers and 135,000 rounds of ammunition. Terrell, *War of the Rebellion,* p. 378. No evidence was found of military plans or activity.
69. Pitman, *Trials for Treason,* p. 12.
70. James G. Blaine, *Twenty Years of Congress,* 2 vols. (Norwich, 1884-1893), I:540.
71. Arthur Bestor, "The American Civil War as a Constitutional Crisis," *American Historical Review* (1964), LXIX: 327.
72. Paul L. Murphy, "Time to Reclaim: The Current Challenge of American Constitutional History," *American Historical Review* (1963), LXIX: 79.
73. Pitman, *Trials for Treason,* p. 68.
74. Hermann Edward von Holst, *Constitutional and Political History of the United States,* 8 vols. (Chicago, 1876), VII:307.
75. Bruce Catton, *U. S. Grant and the American Military Tradition* (Boston, 1954), p. 121.
76. Samuel Klaus, ed., *The Milligan Case* (New York, 1929), p. 34; Milligan's statement to the Huntington County Circuit Court, March 24, 1898; *Herald,* December 15, 1899.
77. L. C. Baker, *History of the United States Secret Service* (Philadelphia, 1867), p. 253; Mogelever, *Baker,* p. 291; Frank L. Klement, *The Copperheads of the Middle West* (Chicago, 1960), p. 240.
78. Joseph Holt, *Report of the Judge Advocate General on "The Order of American Knights" Alias "The Sons of Liberty," A Western Conspiracy in Aid of the Southern Rebellion* (Washington, D.C., 1864). The report was made October 8, 1864, to Secretary of War E. M. Stanton. Randall noted that careful historians do not accept that a dangerous organization opposed the war. James G. Randall, *Civil War and Reconstruction* (Boston, 1937), pp. 389-390.
79. *Herald,* August 24, 1864.
80. Kenneth M. Stampp, "The Milligan Case and the Election of 1864 in Indiana," *Mississippi Valley Historical Review* (1944), XXXI: 53; *Journal,* December 16, 1882.
81. Pitman, *Trials for Treason,* p. 239.
82. Ibid., p. 78.
83. Mayo Fesler, "Secret Political Societies in the North During the Civil War," *Indiana Magazine of History* (1918), XIV: 283.
84. *Herald,* December 7, 1864. Roche was a Democrat. His reputation not only explains why DeLong accepted Roche's testimony but also why Hugh McCulloch gave Roche power of attorney. Bert Anson, "John Roche—Pioneer Irish Businessman," *Indiana Magazine of History* (1959), LV: 53.

85. *Herald,* June 7, 1865.
86. Pitman, *Trials for Treason,* p. 248.
87. Ibid., p. 186.
88. Ibid., p. 166.
89. Ibid., p. 289.
90. Milligan believed that Governor Morton demanded conviction because acquittal would injure the Union cause in the election, and personally pledged to members of the commission that Milligan would not be hurt. Milligan considered it probable that Governor Morton thought President Lincoln promised to disaffirm the finding and set Milligan at liberty when the official record was received. *Herald,* December 15, 1899.
91. *Herald,* July 12, 1865.
92. John A. Marshall, *The American Bastile. A History of the Arbitrary Arrests and Imprisonments . . . during the Late Civil War* (Philadelphia, 1884), pp. 78-89; *Democrat,* December 27, 1866.
93. *Herald,* November 16, 1864.
94. Basler, *Works of Lincoln,* VIII:149.

Chapter IX

Civil Rights Victory

As with the combat infantryman, so with the nation, commitment to battle is the beginning of dying. Then, when the war is over, if death has not terminated the matter, there is the problem of recovery.[1]

As done at other times of great stress, during the Civil War the Supreme Court followed a flexible constitutional interpretation.[2] After the war there was no problem of opposition to Republicans by Democrat judges. This had caused confusion at the beginning of the war in *Ex parte Merryman*.[3] The best-known Democrat judge, Chief Justice Roger Brooke Taney, died in October 1864. Five of the nine judges who comprised the Supreme Court when the civil rights of Milligan were adjudicated had been appointed by President Lincoln.[4]

Unless they were modified or abolished by military necessity, these civil rights, reinforced by an antimilitary tradition, were stated in the Constitution of the United States.[5]

General Hovey was aware of doubts about the authority of the military commission. Furthermore, he was aware that the trials might help the Democrats instead of the Republicans. Consequently he pardoned Andrew Humphreys and sent an explanation to Lincoln: "In my opinion there were two errors committed by the commission, on the trial of Humphreys, which would, before a civil court reverse his case. . . . With a defective record, with the light testimony, and with a strong feeling in the public mind in his favor, I deemed it prudent and politic to release him."[6]

One member of the military commission, William E. McLean, wrote to Lincoln concerning Milligan: "I was compelled to dissent from the findings of the Commission, believing that the evidence adduced wholly failed to sustain the charge of the conspiracy preferred against him. My opinion has not changed since the trial;

and permit me to express the opinion that Mr. Milligan's release from further punishment upon these charges is dictated alike by common justice and the popular sentiment of the people of Indiana."[7]

President Lincoln received such letters and the record of the trial. He talked with people from Indiana. It seemed likely that his action would be similar to that taken before: "When Joseph E. McDonald went to Lincoln about these military trials and asked him not to execute the men convicted in Indiana, who had been convicted by a military commission he said he wouldn't hang them —execute them—but said—I guess I'll keep them in prison awhile to prevent them from killing this Government."[8]

Lincoln did not consider the matter further. But he had gone far enough that Justice David Davis was "satisfied that Lincoln was thoroughly opposed to these military commissions especially in the free states where courts are open—and free."[9]

For Milligan, David Davis was the most important judge appointed to the Supreme Court by President Lincoln. Judge Davis was also on the circuit court for Indiana at Indianapolis. Therefore he knew that at the time of the trial by the military commission the court was open and free.

In 1863, in a charge to a district grand jury, Judge Davis had declared: "We seek to establish the supremacy of the government and to compel submission of the Rebels to the laws. How can we ask them to submit, if we do not ourselves render a willing obedience?"[10]

As Governor Morton's interest in having more control by the state than when there was trial by the military commission made him to some extent in accord with Milligan, so Judge Davis had principles that kept him from completely rejecting Milligan: "The heart of the patriot is sickened and humiliated at the discovery of the frauds and speculations which have been perpetrated upon the Government. It is a matter of the profoundest grief, that there are living among us, those who are base enough to cheat the Government, when the homes of our people are darkened by the horrors of civil war, and our blood and treasure are freely given to save the life of the nation. The loathing and scorn which they

Civil Rights Victory

deservedly receive will not stop the evil. The only effectual way to do it, is to enforce the laws. If men will cheat and defraud in a time like this, they should feel the pressure of the law, and be made, if possible, to disgorge their ill-gotten gains. If subject to the rules and articles of war they should be shot; if in civil life, the severest penalties of the law should be their portion."[11]

Thus the principle of Judge Davis for Milligan, who was in civil life, was to punish with the severest penalty of the law. This was exactly what Milligan wanted because it would give him an opportunity to establish that he was upholding law. But Judge Davis and Judge David McDonald, the other judge on the Circuit Court, stayed clear of Milligan's opposition to the war. In May 1865 Judge McDonald, upon learning of the decision of the military commission, stated that he was "sorry to hear it, not that they are not traitors, but that there is much doubt about their having been convicted by a Court of competent jurisdiction. Judge Davis has the same fears I have on this topic."[12]

The method used in the circuit court, to express their doubts about whether the military commission was a court of competent jurisdiction, was for Judge Davis and Judge McDonald to differ in their views on a writ of habeas corpus so that the case would be sent to the Supreme Court of the United States.

Before circuit court judges could differ on a writ of habeas corpus, Milligan had to get one issued. Also to be remembered is that for the two other Civil War cases dealing with the rights of civilians, *Ex parte Merryman* and *Ex parte Vallandigham,* the Supreme Court did not adjudicate.

Early in the war, *Ex parte Merryman,* a circuit court decision in the district of Maryland, was drafted by Chief Justice Taney when he was on circuit duty. He set forth two main principles: After a civilian was arrested by military authorities, it was their duty to deliver him immediately to civil authorities to be dealt with according to law; only Congress could suspend the writ of habeas corpus.[13]

President Lincoln did not deliver Merryman to civil authorities nor did he accept that only Congress could suspend the writ of habeas corpus. To express opposition to Lincoln, the *Democrat* praised the decision of Taney and proposed to let this question decide whether the United States had a government of constitutional laws or a military dictatorship.[14] However, it was not difficult for DeLong to answer because in an earlier decision Taney admitted that courts were inadequate to deal with rebellion and held that "the President is the fittest person to be entrusted with the responsibility of deciding when an emergency requiring military interposition has arisen."[15]

There was much distrust of Taney[16] by those who wanted to preserve the Union and this distrust extended to the judicial branch of government. Patriotic men in the North rejected court decisions that did not take into consideration the military situation, the loyalty of judges in the civil courts, or the problem of whether Congress was in shape to assume the responsibility of suspending the writ of habeas corpus in case of need.

After the clash with Chief Justice Taney, Lincoln became firmer in his conviction that what he had done and was doing was constitutional. On September 24, 1862, he suspended the writ of habeas corpus and ordered military trials for disloyal civilians. Henceforth he continued to support military commissions. Nevertheless, as Lincoln appointed loyal men to judicial positions, the case became stronger for relying on the courts. The Habeas Corpus Act of March 3, 1863, authorized the president to suspend the privilege of the writ, but also provided that federal courts were to discharge prisoners when a grand jury met and adjourned without taking action against such person.

In the *Prize Cases* in 1863 the Supreme Court sustained acts of President Lincoln, including the blockade. This was a great relief to the Lincoln administration.[17] After that his acts were not seriously questioned.

A circuit court had decided that war necessity prevented the court from interfering with the conviction of Vallandigham by a military commission. Then the case was taken to the Supreme Court, not from the circuit court but directly from the military commission. In *Ex parte Vallandigham* the Supreme Court held that it did not have appellate jurisdiction because the military commission was not a court.[18]

Civil Rights Victory

Ex parte Merryman in a circuit court and *Ex parte Vallandigham* in the Supreme Court made clear what was necessary for a civil rights victory: to proceed legally in order to have the Supreme Court consider the case, and base the case on principles that commanded the support of a majority of the judges. A lasting victory required the enthusiasm of many lawyers, political leaders, and the general public. As Lincoln had stated on June 26, 1857, in connection with the Dred Scott decision: The decision of the Supreme Court "on Constitutional questions, when fully settled, should control, not only the particular cases decided, but the general policy of the country; subject to be disturbed only by amendments of the Constitution as provided in that instrument itself."[19]

Milligan proceeded strictly according to law. A grand jury impaneled by the Federal Circuit Court in Indiana met after Milligan's sentence and adjourned without an indictment against him. He then petitioned the circuit court for a writ of habeas corpus. The problem was placed squarely before Republican judges when his application to be released met all of the terms of the Habeas Corpus Act of March 3, 1863. As the war was nearly over, his legalism had a strong appeal for lawyers. Voluntarily and without pay some of the best legal talent of both political parties worked for Milligan.[20]

Chance almost made legal ability impotent. On April 14, 1865, President Lincoln was assassinated. This stimulated the fear of conspiracy. Those connected with the death of Lincoln were hanged without delaying for a trial in a civil court. President Andrew Johnson approved the death sentence for Milligan. The date was set for May 19, 1865. In order to get execution delayed until there could be a civil trial, it took the efforts of the judges on the circuit court, Governor Morton, and Secretary of War Edwin M. Stanton.[21]

Delay being secured, events favored Milligan. On April 26, 1865, there was the last organized resistance. On May 13, 1865, there was the last fighting. Presumably this ended the war, and Lincoln's suspension of the writ of habeas corpus was only until the end of the war. The provisions of the Habeas Corpus Act of 1863 had not been carried out enough to make any difference in the matter of arrest, confinement, and punishment of political prisoners. But it was different with the end of the war and the principles of Judge Davis.[22]

Personal considerations also favored Milligan: "I owe the commutation of my sentence to Secretary of War Edwin M. Stanton . . . Mr. Stanton and I were early friends. We were both admitted to the practice of law at the same bar and he had been a frequent visitor at my house while I was still a resident of Ohio."[23] It was Stanton who issued the order for the commutation of the sentence and President Johnson approved.[24] However, Stanton insisted on martial law in the conquered Confederacy.[25]

Furthermore, as was stated to Governor Morton, it would do the "party no good to shed more blood but on the contrary, if we are merciful, the child is not yet born who will see the defeat of the Republican party, whilst on the other hand, if we are not, the reaction will come and probably the coming year will witness our overthrow."[26]

Thus the Supreme Court case *Ex parte Milligan* was the result of personal, political, and legal factors. In court the legal factors controlled. To be sure, the Chief Justice of the Supreme Court after Taney, Salmon P. Chase, as well as other justices, had been active in politics to support President Lincoln. But what had been favored when in politics was commonly declared illegal when considered from the standpoint of a judge interpreting the Constitution.[27]

Since the military commission that sentenced Milligan to be hanged had functioned under the authority of President Lincoln, the justification of what was done followed his reasoning. In August 1864 General Benjamin F. Butler had received from President Lincoln a statement of the principle to be followed: "Nothing justifies the suspending of the civil by the military authority, but military necessity, and of the existence of that necessity the military commander, and not a popular vote, is to decide."[28]

In *Ex parte Milligan,* Butler reasoned that the courts in Indiana were open only because the military protected them: "It has been said that martial law, and its execution by trials by military commission, is fatal to liberty and the pursuit of happiness; but we

Civil Rights Victory

are only asking for the exercise of military power, when necessity demands and prudence dictates . . . when the law is silent; when justice is overthrown; when the life of the nation is threatened . . . martial law may prevail, so that civil law may again live, to the end that this may be a 'government of laws and not of men.' "[29]

James A. Garfield, a Republican, and Jeremiah Sullivan Black, a Democrat, presented the argument in favor of Milligan. Garfield reasoned that to be "handed over to the civil authorities for trial is precisely what they petitioned for, and what, according to the laws of Congress, should have been done."[30]

Black continued, "We submit that a person not in the military or naval service cannot be punished at all until he has a fair, open, public trial before an impartial jury, in an ordained and established court, to which jurisdiction has been given by law to try him for that specific offence." Since a military commission was not regulated by law and could not be regulated, "It asserts the right of the executive government, without the intervention of the judiciary, to capture, imprison, and kill any person to whom that government or its paid dependents may choose to impute an offence."[31]

A unanimous Supreme Court decision held that under the Habeas Corpus Act of 1863 the Federal Circuit Court at Indianapolis had jurisdiction. Justice Davis wrote the decision. The argument that it was necessary to try Milligan by the military commission collapsed when confronted with a civil court whose judges had as strong a claim to loyalty as the army officers.

As Judge Davis stated, "This court has judicial knowledge that in Indiana the Federal authority was always unopposed, and its courts always open to hear criminal accusations and redress grievances."[32] The basic constitutional principle was that "The Constitution of the United States is a law for rulers and people, equally in war and in peace, and covers with the shield of its protection all classes of men, at all times, and under all circumstances." Consequently, "Martial rule can never exist where the courts are open, and in the proper and unobstructed exercise of their jurisdiction."[33]

Although the decision was unanimous so far as civil trial was concerned, four judges held that Congress had the power, although not exercised, to authorize the military commission. Outside of the Supreme Court there also was uncertainty. Some thought it was no longer the president but Congress that was challenged by the majority decision,[34] that the verdict of the court-martial accomplished its purpose to expose traitors long before the Supreme Court decision.[35]

Practical politics weakened the constitutional principle on which the judges were unanimous. It was soon questioned in connection with military rule in the South. There persisted the conclusion that those who drafted and ratified the Constitution intended to provide a broad range of executive power.[36]

Nevertheless, *Ex parte Milligan* became well known as the leading case in which the Supreme Court found the president beyond his legal power in the exercise of domestic prerogative. A generation of young lawyers read the flaming language of Judge Davis. Democrats supplemented this with the oratory of Jeremiah Sullivan Black.[37] From this emerged the tradition that the president and military action based on the war power was limited.[38] Also, relevant to *Ex parte Milligan* is the thinking of scholars who have considered it proper to criticize those in authority and have rejected censure in the name of patriotism.[39]

Except for the Civil War period President Lincoln's thinking favored such a tradition. On April 11, 1865, in his last speech, concerned mainly with the problem of the Radical Republicans,[40] he indicated that after the war he expected the termination of emergency powers.[41]

Denunciation of *Ex parte Milligan* was by the Radical Republicans, especially Congressmen Thad Stevens, whom Milligan had earlier considered to be the only man in Congress to have proper legal understanding that the relationship with the South was war. Stevens thought that the majority of the Supreme Court, as well as President Johnson, threatened military control of the South.[42]

Determined to have military control of the South, Congress authorized trial and punishment by military commission, as four of the judges had thought proper in *Ex parte Milligan*. To make doubly sure, Congress used its authority to limit the jurisdiction of the Supreme Court and thus prevent any case involving this

Civil Rights Victory

question from reaching the court. Lincoln worshipers kept the facts of Milligan's fight for civil liberty out of Lincoln biographies and school histories.[43] Thus, as Milligan had expected, precedent soon began to prove its strength.

In time those who championed Lincoln found a way to accept *Ex parte Milligan*. As one author stated, "It is well, however, that we consider Lincoln and his methods for meeting emergencies as one outstanding exception in our history . . . we need the inspiration of Lincoln's greatness; but we need also the restraint of law backed by an alert public opinion."[44]

However, later wars showed that the restraint of law weakened as the situation became less favorable for the security of the United States. The precedents of President Lincoln to win a war, and of Congress to keep the war won, have received more attention during crises than the principles stated by Judge Davis. Arousing the fear of conspiracy, when there has been no dangerous conspiracy, has continued to threaten government based on the right reason of law.[45]

When Milligan was released from prison at Columbus, Ohio, on April 10, 1866, the *Democrat* hailed this as the first triumph over a military commission.[46] But what would happen to Milligan after he had been accused of being a traitor and convicted by a military commission? A survey of traitors shows that "it seems a constant in the history of nations that the betrayor of his country leaves no memories save those of disgust and contempt. . . . The people he seeks to ruin look upon him with indignation and outrage. The enemy for whom he works has nothing but contempt for him."[47]

DeLong expected that Milligan would have a civil trial.[48] He was indicted in the Circuit Court and his bond was set at five thousand dollars. But the willingness of DeLong to place Milligan where he had the possibility of a legal victory on the accusation of being a traitor was not shared by those who controlled the courts. Milligan regularly attended the federal court demanding a trial. He could not get one.[49] Instead, the case was dismissed.

Except for not being able to get a civil trial, the situation favored Milligan. After being in prison for eighteen months, he arrived in Huntington on April 12, 1866, and received one of the greatest ovations ever given to a citizen of Indiana. Mayor William C. Kocher welcomed him "once more to your home, to mingle with your family and these people who have so long, and so well known you, and who have long since looked upon you as a man of eminent legal ability, a statesman, and one who has ever been true to the Constitution and laws of this country." Milligan's words in reply revealed the stamp of the man: The testimonial by neighbors was a proof that "it is not the acts or words of others that can degrade a man, but that each must stand upon the basis of his own manhood."[50]

A few soldiers who did not share the sentiments of Kocher stood with "clenched fists and whitened faces." But they were silent. The thoughts that went through their minds were probably not so favorable as those of DeLong for Milligan: "While few doubted of his guilt, yet many, at the time, doubted the rights to try him" by military commission.[51] However, so firm was the grip of Milligan on the Democrats in Huntington County that they had no demonstration of welcome when General Slack returned to Huntington with a good war record. Nor did Republicans welcome a War Democrat.[52]

What the future would hold was presaged when Milligan made a speech on May 26, 1866, at Bluffton. He defended state rights and civil rights, as he reminded them was done in his Fort Wayne speech: the " 'war power' asserted and exercised by the late administration is more dangerous than all, and is wholly inconsistent with the very idea of constitutional government, is at war with the spirit of civil liberty, and subversive of all good order." The West and South had common interests: "There is an aristocracy of crime warmed into life by the protective system extended to New England capital, controlling Congress, as the East India company did the Parliament of England—controlling it with money."[53]

Then Milligan declared: "God is just! But to us who do not understand his province that Justice sometimes seems tardy. I never was prone to a belief in frequent occurrence of special provinces, but among the greatest sinners against God's righteous will was a Lincoln, a Brough, and a Morton. One has been summon-

Civil Rights Victory 105

ed to the bar of retributive justice with his sins unrepented. Another covered all over with the mildew of debauchery and wrapped in the exhalations from which buzzard will turn their offended noses, carried to the grave the impress of infamy. There yet remains one of the Godless trio; but the plague is on its westward march, his limbs are smote with the blight of crime and tremble under their load of corruption, but I pray that he may live long enough to realize in this world rather than in the next that God is just. But he who cannot see the hand of divine interposition in the visitation upon these wicked men deserves to be damned for want of faith."[54]

As with former speeches of Milligan, Republican newspapers quoted the invective of "Major General Milligan."[55] This placed the Democrats on the defensive. Although it could be said that "history gives no instance of a cure, pronounced upon a foe, under greater provocation."[56] this did not change what DeLong observed: the Democrat party rejected Milligan.[57]

He returned full time to his law practice,[58] and again became one of the leading lawyers in northern Indiana.[59] Unable to get a civil trial, he began lawsuits against those involved in his arrest. The delay, expense, and failure to reach any satisfactory conclusion did more to further the reasoning of President Lincoln than that of Milligan. He could content himself when the court decided in his favor. President Lincoln had to act.

Congress had been aware that probably civil suits would be brought after the war and passed the Indemnity Act of 1863. This was amended in 1866. It protected military and civil officials who made arrests. As viewed by the *Democrat,* Congress protected "the lawless faction which ruled the country with a rod of vengeance during the last five years."[60]

But officials were not completely protected. Consequently Milligan sued Slack and twenty-three others for $500,000 damages caused by trespass and false imprisonment.[61] Milligan contended that the statements made against him in the trial before the military commission at Indianapolis were false, scandalous, defamatory, and libelous. He listed the charges made against him and concluded that he had been falsely, maliciously, and without probable cause accused of civil and military crimes. He maintained that he always had been a true and patriotic citizen of Indiana.

As the case proceeded, some of the names were dropped. On May 6, 1871, the case was *nolle prosequi* as to Slack. Hovey became the main defendant.

General Hovey had been the commander of the Indiana Military District and had appointed the military commission. He was the one who told Milligan he had no civil rights. Then the military commission had denied a separate trial and held Milligan guilty because he was considered to be a member of the Sons of Liberty, not because of what he had done himself. This was in spite of the testimony of John Roche (confirmed by Milligan under oath at the time of the civil trial) that Milligan was not a member of any secret organization in 1864.

In the United States Circuit Court, Hovey had in his favor that he acted under the authority of President Lincoln. Nevertheless, he had to face the questions of civil rights, the competency of the civil court, whether there had been a great conspiracy, and whether Milligan was innocent.

Milligan v. *Hovey*, as the case was called after Slack's name was dropped, developed into one aspect of political party battles. Thomas Hendricks was a counsel for Milligan. Hendricks terminated his services as United States Senator in 1869, was elected governor of Indiana in 1872, and became vice-president of the United States in 1884. He had strong personal convictions because of his opposition to military arrests and trials. Benjamin Harrison was a counsel for Hovey. Harrison had been a brigadier general of volunteers and was elected president of the United States in 1888. He had strong personal convictions because he believed that the military commission had acted in good faith to save the Union.

The exposition of the law to the jury by Judge Thomas Drummond included comments on the civil court, the conspiracy, and Milligan. The law was what had been stated in *Ex parte Milligan:* "Martial law cannot arise from a threatened invasion. The necessity must be actual and present; the invasion real, such as effectually closes the courts and deposes the civil administration." As for Indiana, "We know judicially, and therefore it is proved, that

Civil Rights Victory

the federal courts of Indiana were open during the time the events occurred which gave rise to this controversy."[62]

Although the courts were open, "It is claimed that there was a great conspiracy pervading the state, having for its end a revolution, civil and military, in the interest of the enemies of the government. But, in fact, only a few were arrested, and tried before the military commission, and it cannot admit of question that the plaintiff could have been taken by civil officers before the courts, and there tried for any offense of which he had been guilty."[63]

As for Milligan, "If you should believe there is any evidence connecting the plaintiff with a conspiracy against the government, though it would not justify his trial by a military commission, yet it would undoubtedly affect your conclusions upon the question of damages; so, too, if you should believe the acts of the defendants were done without sufficient excuse, and the plaintiff was an innocent man."[64]

The jury was also instructed to consider that some members of the Sons of Liberty, "how many does not appear—were engaged in a treasonable design against the government, and that their purpose was to involve the whole of the society, if possible; if not, then all they could influence in that design. The military authorities here at the time had knowledge of this scheme, and under the belief that it was indispensable to thwart it at once, arrested some of the supposed leaders, and among the rest the plaintiff. Under the conviction produced by this state of things the defendants arrested, tried and condemned the plaintiff upon the evidence before them. Whether the evidence or what might have been produced would have warranted his conviction before a civil court need not be decided. It is clear that the defendants were performing what they considered a military duty."[65]

The verdict of the jury was for Milligan with nominal damages. He was awarded five dollars. Costs of fifteen hundred dollars were charged to the defendants. The *Herald* proposed that Congress should vote payment of the amount and it was believed in Huntington that this was done.[66]

Milligan and those who favored him claimed a victory. Military trials of civilians ended in the North. In the specialized histories of lawyers Milligan became established as a leading lawyer. U.S. Lesh wrote a novel in which Milligan was the hero.[67]

Milligan's integrity enabled him to close his career with personal victory. Ovation began with lawyers when he resigned from the bar and made the statement quoted in the preface of my essay. When he died the next year, the Republican and the Democrat local newspapers honored him. Milligan reaped some of the rewards of the philosophy of those legal writers in the United States before 1860 who made no concessions to "necessity."[68]

NOTES

1. For 24,416 Hoosiers who had been killed or died the matter was terminated. Arville L. Funk, *Hoosiers in the Civil War* (Chicago, 1967), p. 3.
2. Edward A. Purcell, Jr., "American Jurisprudence between the Wars: Legal Realism and the Crisis of Democratic Theory," *American Historical Review* (1969), LXXV: 446.
3. Walker Lewis, *Without Fear of Favor: A Biography of Chief Justice Roger Brooke Taney* (Boston, 1965), p. 464. The confusion went back at least as far as the Dred Scott decision. Joseph G. Gambone, "Ex parte Milligan: The Restoration of Judicial Prestige?" *Civil War History* (1970), XVI: 259.
4. David M. Silver, *Lincoln's Supreme Court* (Urbana, 1956), p. 232.
5. Amendment V; Arthur A. Ekrich, Jr., *The Civilian and the Military* (New York, 1956), p. 98.
6. Hovey to Lincoln, January 10, 1865, in Roy Basler, ed., *The Collected Works of Abraham Lincoln*, 9 vols. (New Brunswick, 1953-1955), VIII:211.
7. Huntington, Indiana, *Democrat,* June 7, 1866.
8. David Davis to Herndon, September 19, 1866. H-W papers; William H. Herndon and Jesse William Weik, *Herndon's Lincoln: The True Story of a Great Life,* 3 vols. (Chicago, 1889), p. 556.
9. David Davis to Herndon, September 19, 1866. H-W papers.
10. *Democrat,* May 14, 1863.
11. Ibid., May 21, 1863.
12. Donald O. Dewey, ed., "Hoosier Justice: The Journal of David McDonald, 1864-1868," *Indiana Magazine of History* (1966),

Civil Rights Victory

LXII: 203. The judges were under pressure from those who denounced as "an ally of the enemy" anyone who opposed a military commission. Willard L. King, *Lincoln's Manager: David Davis* (Cambridge, 1960), p. 203.
13. Federal Cases of the United States, Ex parte *Merryman* (1861), 17: 144.
14. *Democrat,* June 6, 1861.
15. Huntington, Indiana, *Herald,* July 3, 1861.
16. George D. Braden, "The Search for Objectivity in Constitutional Law," *Yale Law Journal* (1947-1948), 57: 574.
17. J. G. Randall, *Lincoln the President: Midstream* (New York, 1952), p. 154; Habeas Corpus Act, March 3, 1863 in *U.S. Statutes at Large,* Thirty-Seventh Congress, Session III (1863). Other provisions of the act were that a list of political prisoners was to be furnished to the judges of the United States courts, prisoners were to be discharged only after taking an oath of allegiance, the order of the President was a defense to any action for false arrest, and that the suit might be carried to the Supreme Court.
18. U.S. Supreme Court, Vol. 68, I, Wallace (1863), 243.
19. Basler, *Works of Lincoln,* II:401; Don E. Fehrenbacher, "Lincoln and Judicial Supremacy: A Note on the Galena Speech of July 23, 1856," *Civil War History* (1970), XVI: 204.
20. U.S. Statutes at Large, Thirty-seventh Congress, Session III (1863), p. 755; U.S. Supreme Court, Vol. 71, 4 Wallace (1866), 116; Alexander Harris, *A Review of the Political Conflict in America* (New York, 1876), p. 460.
21. King, *David Davis,* p. 250.
22. Bowles and Horsey were included but Milligan supplied the determination. *The Nation,* January 10, 1867; James G. Randall, *Constitutional Problems under Lincoln* (New York, 1926), p. 166.
23. *Herald,* December 15, 1899.
24. Ibid.
25. Benjamin P. Thomas and Harold M. Hyman, *Stanton: The Life and Times of Lincoln's Secretary of War* (New York, 1962), p. 477.
26. Silas F. Miller to O. P. Morton, May 12, 1865, in Harvey Wish, ed., "Civil War Letters and Despatches," *Indiana Magazine of History* (1937), XXXIII: 71.
27. John G. Nicolay and John Hay, *Abraham Lincoln: A History,* 10 vols. (New York, 1890), IX:401.
28. Basler, *Works of Lincoln,* VII: 488.
29. U.S. Supreme Court, Vol. 71 (1866), 4 Wallace, Ex parte *Milligan,* 101, 106.
30. Ibid., 61. Garfield had been a major general. At the time of the

trial he was a congressman from Ohio. Later he was president of the United States.
31. Ibid., 83.
32. Ibid., 121.
33. Ibid., 120, 127.
34. "Milligan Case," *American Law Review* (1867), I: 38.
35. Logan Esarey, *History of Indiana from Its Exploration to 1922*, 4 vols. (Dayton, 1924), II:791.
36. Edward S. Corwin, *The President: Office and Powers* (New York, 1948), pp. 15-16.
37. William D. Lewis, ed., *Great American Lawyers*, 8 vols. (Philadelphia, 1907-1909), VI:52. Black, attorney general for President Buchanan, was the Democrat spokesman for trial by jury.
38. Russell F. Weigley, *History of the United States Army* (New York, 1967); John P. Roche, *Shadow and Substance: Essays on the Theory and Structure of Politics* (New York, 1964), p. 136.
39. J. Allen Smith, *The Growth and Decadence of Constitutional Government* (New York, 1930), p. 267. There were unsuccessful attempts to silence both Vernon L. Parrington and Charles A. Beard.
40. T. Harry Williams, *Lincoln and the Radicals* (Madison, 1965), p. 370.
41. Basler, *Works of Lincoln*, VIII:402.
42. Harold M. Hyman, "Johnson, Stanton, and Grant: A Reconsideration of the Army's Role in the Events Leading to Impeachment," *American Historical Review* (1960), LXVI: 89.
43. James Douglas Anderson, "The Facts of the Milligan Case," *Tyler's Quarterly and Genealogical Magazine* (1948), XXIX: 260.
44. Kenneth A. Bernard, "Lincoln and Civil Liberties," *Abraham Lincoln Quarterly* (1951), VI: 399.
45. Clinton Rossiter, *The Supreme Court and the Commander in Chief* (Ithaca, 1951), p. 131; Samuel P. Huntington, *The Soldier and the State: The Theory and Practice of Civil Military Relations* (Cambridge, 1957), p. 3; David Brion Davis, *The Fear of Conspiracy* (Ithaca, 1971), p. 362.
46. *Democrat*, April 12, 1866.
47. George Fort Milton, *Abraham Lincoln and the Fifth Column* (New York, 1942), p. 333.
48. *Herald*, April 4, 1866; ibid., May 30, 1866.
49. *Democrat*, June 7, 1866; ibid., December 13, 1866.
50. Ibid., April 19, 1866.
51. *Herald*, April 18, 1866.
52. Ibid., May 30, 1866.
53. *Democrat*, May 31, 1866. This speech, printed in full in the

Civil Rights Victory

    Democrat, was seven columns long.
54. Ibid.
55. *Herald,* June 6, 1866.
56. *Democrat,* June 28, 1866.
57. *Herald,* June 20, 1866; Logansport, Indiana, *Democratic Pharos,* June 13, 1866.
58. In 1883 he got little support to be a state senator. The most severe condemnation of Milligan as a politician, while holding him in high regard as a lawyer, came from his friend and neighbor Thomas Marshall. Thomas R. Marshall, *Recollections: A Hoosier Salad* (Indianapolis, 1925), p. 73. As long as Milligan lived he was a source of bitter division within the community. To one faction he was a hero, to the other he was a traitor. Huntington, Indiana, *Herald-Press,* May 13, 1964.
59. *Herald,* January 5, 1900. One of the signs of his prosperity was an oil painting mentioned in the will. It is not known by the Huntington County Historical Society where this painting is located.
60. *Democrat,* May 10, 1866.
61. Huntington County Court of Common Pleas, *Milligan v. Slack et al.* (1868), Federal Records Center, Chicago, No. 1472. The best known other men were Oliver P. Morton and Alvin P. Hovey.
62. Federal Cases of the United States, *Milligan v. Hovey* (1871), 17: 381.
63. Ibid.
64. Ibid., 383.
65. Ibid.
66. *Herald-Press,* May 13, 1864.
67. U.S. Lesh, *A Knight of the Golden Circle* (Boston, 1911); John C. Cochrane, "Arbitrary Arrests in Indiana During the Civil War with Special Reference to the Milligan Case," Masters Thesis (Indiana University, 1917); Gilbert R. Tredway, "Indiana Against the Administration, 1861-1865," Ph.D. dissertation (Indiana University, 1962).
68. Maxwell Bloomfield, "Law vs. Politics: The Self-Image of the American Bar (1830-1860)," *American Journal of Legal History* (1968), XII: 319.

Appendix

STATEMENT BY MILLIGAN AT THE TRIAL OF ALEXANDER J. DOUGLAS
(Cincinnati, May 29, 1863)

In the statement of the reasons why the defendant should be discharged, I shall refer to those exculpatory circumstances in evidence in the case, as well as that which the law requires the Court to notice, only as tend to negative the idea of malice. And I use the term "malice" in its legal sense as applied to the order for the alleged violation of which the arrest was made and this proceeding instituted. I assume that in this case as in other actions for words, the gist of the action is malice or evil intent. And although adjudicated precedents are somewhat rare, owing to the fact that the existence and sittings of such tribunals have not been frequent in the history of our country. In all actions for words, whether civil or criminal, the truth may be given in evidence to rebut the presumption of malice raised by the speaking of the words. To a lawyer, precedents, when in point, are more forcible than abstract logic. As one nearest in point because enacted to effect the same object, I refer the commission to the Act of Congress of 1798, known as the Sedition Act, which allowed the truth of the words to be given in evidence, (hoping that the order under which we are proceeding will not be less liberal.) Not only so, but in some actions for words the defendant will be allowed to show the existence of a general rumor and that the charges were believed in the neighborhood.

And Courts *ex officio* will take notice of matters of history. Therefore the propriety of referring to such matters of general notoriety as form a part of the history we are now making in justifica-

Statement by Milligan

tion of the offensive words proven, if the Commission thinks that any such were proven, with me admits of no question. Now, it is not to be concealed that there are two parties in the country; one friendly to the Administration and the other distrustful. Nor is it to be expected that those who oppose the Administration will have the same confidence in the wisdom of its policy or the integrity of its purpose as its friends and supporters.

We have been taught that "eternal vigilance is the price of liberty;" and a jealous watchfulness of those in power necessary and right. And it has long since become a habit of our people, and any restraint of that habit is calculated to chafe and irritate them. And there are restrictions which to the friends of the Administration might awake no alarm, but be regarded as necessary to restrain the licentiousness of free thought and free speech; while to those whose feelings of antagonism incite a keener apprehension of danger they might be cause of greatest alarm. Now whether the remarks were made about the Administration or the Republican party, upon which the witnesses are about equally divided, I think, should make but little difference, when we consider what is usually understood by the Administration. Not only those who execute, but Congress who make the laws (for it cannot be overlooked that there are those outside of the army who seek not only to control the army but the President and the whole country), are included in the term Administration. And well might the remark be made of them that they were doing more to suppress free speech than to suppress the rebellion by the clamor they were raising and the strife they were creating. But for the sake of argument I will assume that it was spoken of the Administration. Now, is there not much in the circumstances surrounding the case to warrant the expression and rebut the presumption of malice. There are certain axioms, the truth of which are no longer debatable. Example: "In union there is strength." A rational being never acts without a motive, and the action and motive are correlatives reflecting each other. The opinions of honest men are not always matters of choice, but are convictions forced upon them by evidenciary circumstances which to them at least seem sufficient. To conceal those opinions is a restraint upon the freedom of thought, to which the American people are not yet habituated. But on the contrary, have been in the habit of thinking that even "error might be tolerated while reason was left free to combat it"; and in this spirit were the remarks of the defendant made, that the Administration were doing more to suppress free speech than the rebellion; or, those words, the present "Administration is endeavoring to bring the people under military law so as to deprive them of the right of suffrage." Because to the mind of the defendant the party having the conducting of the war, the President, the Congress, the Cabinet, and leading Republican politicians were doing that which the defendant was unable to reconcile with an intention on their part to restore the Government, or put down the rebellion. Because through their public journals, public speakers and otherwise, they were continually doing that which could have no other rational effect than to divide and weaken the forces of the North, by charging the Democratic portion of it with treasonable designs, when they knew they had none; and doing that which would necessarily unite and strengthen the rebels by an ever irritating clamor about their habits and institutions, and that often repeated and false report, carried to the rebel lines in Republican journals, "that the Democratic party in the North sympathized with the rebels and their cause." These with the restrictions imposed by the military, with to him an apparent want of power to make, and necessity for their existence, together with their dangerous tendency then anticipated by many, and now realized in a feverish solicitude all over the country. These and like indices pointing to an event so apparent, and not being a mere succession of accidents having no impelling motive or attracting object, but being so well adapted to that end, and none other, justly seemed to intercept all hope of a restoration of our Government. And these views if justly entertained, were a sufficient reason for the remark that he "thanked God that the widows and orphans could not look to him and say he was the cause of the war, &c." The evidence in this case is by no means satisfactory. The conflict in the evidence of the witnesses for accusation of itself, should admonish the commission to receive the same with great caution. And when we take into consideration the fact, that they are in every material point contradicted by the witnesses for the defendant, that

Statement by Milligan

caution should be the more vigilant. The feelings and bias of the principal witnesses for the accusation, the circumstances under which the evidence is given, the uncertainty of a correct conception of what was said, the versatility of understanding and unconscious translation of defendant's words into their own dialect as witnessed in the variety of expressions of the same idea by the different witnesses, warn us how easy injustice might be done to the defendant. Then again the circumstances under which the speech of Mr. Douglas was made is full of admonitory incidents, not to say charitable relations. He was there not as one of the speakers, but by mere accident, had been in the neighborhood attending the wedding of his brother.

Mr. Vallandigham was the advertised speaker. The news of whose arrest was fresh and exciting and it could not be expected that the people would readily acquiesce in a proceeding so rare, and to them full of seeming danger; and in an extemporaneous speech, tempered in some degree at least by the feelings of a community that felt intensely on the subject, that Mr. Douglas should utter sentiments that to this commission might seem out of place, is not to be wondered at; nor does it furnish any evidence that he expressed sympathy for those in arms against the Government of the United States; nor that he declared disloyal sentiments and opinions with the object of discouraging enlistments, inciting resistance to the laws, giving aid and comfort to the enemy, and weakening the powers of the Government in its efforts to suppress an unlawful rebellion.

As to the specification charging the words "our once glorious Government is aiming to build up a despotism," &c., I know Mr. Douglas could not have uttered such a sentiment, because he recognizes no Government as *ours* whose powers are not founded on the constitution of the United States, the principles of which are rendered more sacred and glorious by the perils to which its votaries are daily exposed.

In conclusion, I am impelled to remind the Commission that the accusation has failed to prove even the substance of any set of words charged, or enough of all when taken together in the connection in which they were spoken, to convict the defendant of a single sentiment or emotion inconsistent with the deepest devotion to the interest, fame and perpetuity of our Government, the laws and institutions of our common country. And I cannot but believe that this arrest is the result of a misconception on the part of the witnesses of the facts and legal import of the case, and that the prosecution would never have been instituted had the department been advised of the facts in the case and, therefore, ask that the defendant be discharged.

Index

Abolitionism, 16, 23, 24, 49, 52, 73, 75
Act of Congress of 1798, 76, 112
Adams, Henry, 28
Adams, John Quincy, 23
Allen, William J., 54
American Revolution, 21, 28, 39, 60, 61, 66
Army of the Potomac, 59
Articles of Confederation, 21, 77
Atlanta, occupation of, 68, 82

Bates, Edward, 62
Bingham, J. J., 81, 85; arrested, 85
Black, Jeremiah Sullivan, 101, 102
Bowles, W. A., 87
Breckinridge, Samuel M., 64
British Empire, 28
Brough, 104
Brown, John, 38
Buchanan, James, 24
Burnett, Judge Advocate Major H. L., 87, 88
Burnside, Major General Ambrose E., 83
Burr, Aaron, 48
Butler, General Benjamin F., 100

Calhoun, John C., 11
Cameron, Simon, 37
Carrington, Henry B., 66
Castleman, John B., 64
Chamberlain, L. B., 37
Change from practice, principle of, 9
Chase, Salmon P., 100
Clay, Henry, 24

Coffroth, John R., 49, 62, 74, 75, 82, 83, 84, 88
Coke, Sir Edward, 21
Colonial charters, 9
Common law, 18
Congress of 1690, 26
Congress of 1775, 27
Conner, A. H., 41
Continental Congress of 1774, 26
Convention of 1754, 26
Cooley, Thomas M., 26
Copperheads, 45
Coventry, Sir Thomas, 21

Dailey, D. O., 89
Davis, David, 35, 41, 96, 97, 100, 101, 102, 103
Davis, Jefferson, 11, 73
De Tocqueville, Alexis, 27
Declaration of Independence, 21, 27, 77
DeLong, Alexander, 18, 36-41, 47, 61-68, 78, 83-89, 98, 103, 104; reaction to Milligan, 40; support of Lincoln, 38-41
DeLong, Isaac, 37, 47
Democrat (newspaper), xi, 18, 21, 22, 23, 24, 25, 37, 38, 41, 45, 47, 51, 52, 53, 54, 73, 75, 76, 77, 81, 82, 85, 86, 97, 103, 104
Democrat party, viii, xi, 3, 6, 7, 15-17, 18, 20, 24-26, 33, 36-38, 39, 41, 45, 47, 49, 50-52, 53, 60, 61, 63, 64, 66-68, 73-88, 95, 101, 104, 114
Democratic State Committee, 81

117

Dodd, Harrison H., 47, 67, 79, 80, 84, 85, 86, 87, 88; arrested, 69, 81; as Grand Commander of Knights, 81; trial of, 68-69
Douglas, Alexander J., 75-77, 112, 115; arrested, 76
Douglas, Stephen A., 24, 25, 27, 39; support of Lincoln, 24
Dred Scott decision, 99
Drummond, Thomas, 106

East India Company, 104
Election of 1863, 75
Eleventh Congressional District, 3, 52
Emancipation Proclamation, 36
Ex parte Merryman, 95, 97, 99
Ex parte Milligan, 100, 102, 103, 106
Ex parte Vallandigham, 97, 98, 99
Executive Council, 10, 65

Federalists, 39, 66
Fifth Amendment, 22
First Amendment, 18
Fort Sumter, assault on, 24, 33, 45
Fort Wayne Speech (1864), 47, 49, 81, 82, 87, 104
47th Regiment, 25, 66
Fremont, John C., 35

Garfield, James A., viii, 101
Garrison, William Lloyd, 37
Giddings, Joshua R., 37
Good, General, 81
Grant, Ulysses S., 59, 67, 69, 81, 82
Great Britain, 9, 21, 23, 26, 27, 104

Habeas corpus, writ of, viii, 22, 49, 60, 61, 65, 73, 76, 97, 99; suspension of, 52, 62, 63, 98, 99
Habeas Corpus Act of 1863, 98, 99, 101
Hanna, Judge, 79
Harrison, Benjamin, 106
Hascall, Brigadier General Milo S., 73

Heffren, H., 87
Hendricks, Thomas A., 47, 52, 73, 106
Henry, Patrick, 22
Hooker, Major General Joseph, 59
Hoosier Democracy, 15
Horsey, Stephen, 87
Horton, T., 40-41; arrested, 40
Hovey, Major General Alvin P., 64, 69, 95, 106
Humphreys, Andrew, 87, 95; pardoned, 95
Huntington County: October 1862 elections, 41, 53; political situation in, 36; race problems, 41; surge of patriotism, 39
Huntington County Democrat Convention (1862), 54
Huntington *Herald* (newspaper), xi, 18, 36, 37, 38, 41, 50, 75, 107

Indemnity Act of 1863, 104
Indiana: Hoosier Democracy, 15; November 1862 elections, 41; opposition to Lincoln, 19; political situation in, 36; state constitution, 17
Indiana Military District, 106
Indiana Supreme Court, 77
Indiana Volunteers, 87
Indianapolis *Daily State Sentinel*, 85
Intent of those who drafted the law, principle of, 9

Jackson, Andrew, 10, 12, 24, 25, 38, 64, 65, 67; Farewell Address, 23
Jacobs, Richard T., 85
Jefferson, Thomas, 22, 23, 24, 64, 65, 74, 77; on state sovereignty, 9
Johnson, Andrew, viii, 99, 100, 102
Johnson, General Joseph E., 81

Knights (secret organization), 78, 81, 88
Kocher, William C., 45, 104

Index

Leavitt, Judge, 76
Lee, General Robert E., 67
Lesh, U.S., xi, 6, 108
Lincoln, Abraham, and Allen, 54; answer to Morton's letter, 83, attitude toward slavery, 35; background of, 6-8, assassination of, viii, 99; call for volunteers, 33; and Castleman arrest, 63; clash with Taney, 98; Coffroth speech and, 75; compared to Milligan, 6-8; concept of American law, 33; *Democrat's* review of, 72-73; De-Long's support of, 38-41; on Dred Scott decision, 99; economic measures of, 52; in House of Representatives, 33; in Illinois legislature, 33; Inaugural Address (1861), 33; inaugurated, 10; Indiana opposition to, 20; instructions to Schofield, 62-63; and Jacobs, 85; letter to Butler, 100; and McLean, 95-96; and Merryman, 97; message to Congress (1861), 34-35; New York City speech (1861), 33; Northern support of, 33-34; renomination of, 63; military trial of civilians and, 35, 60-61, 83; Supreme Court appointments, 95, 96; use of patronage, 33; world opinion of, 6
Lincoln Proclamation (1862), 25, 86
Locke, John, 9, 21
Louisiana Purchase, 9

Macauley, Lord, 21
McClellan, General George B., 52, 82, 83, 89; nominated for President, 82
McCulloch, Hugh, 27
McDonald, Joseph E., 79, 80, 89, 96
McDowell, James F., 52
McLean, William E., 95-96
Madison, James, 23, 25, 77

Magna Carta, 20
Martial law, 74
Mexican War, 17
Military Commission (Indianapolis), 88
Milligan, Lambdin P.: arrested, viii, 3, 22, 83, 84, 85; attitude toward Negroes, 16; background of, 3, 6-8; Bluffton speech, 104-5; as chairman for Huntington County, 50; Circuit Court indictment, 103; civil suit against Slack, 104-7; and Coffroth, 62, 74-75, 82, 83, 84, 88; compared to Lincoln, 6-8; as council for Douglas, 76-77, 112-16; Copperhead epithet, 45; and Dailey, 89; death of, 107; and Dodd, 79, 80-81, 84, 86, 87, 88; election of 1863, 75; encounter with Slack, 25-26; final statement to Huntington County Bar, xi; Fort Wayne Speech (1864), 47, 81, 82, 87, 104; as gubernatorial candidate, 78-81; imprisoned, 89; interpretation of Tenth Amendment, 8; invective of, 37, 48; and McLean, 95; and Morton, 84; National Convention delegate, 82; in National Guard of Ohio, 13; and Northern Democrats, 78; opinion of Lincoln administration, 48; petition for writ of habeas corpus, 99; political techniques of, 7; public opinion toward, 6; rejection by Indiana Democrats, 79-83, 104; and Roche, 89; at Soldier's Home (Indianapolis), 89; and Sons of Liberty, 67; and Southern Democrats, 78; and Stanton, 99, 100; state convention (1862), 51-52; on state sovereignty, vii, 79; trial of, viii, 3, 86-89; and Zumro, 86
Milligan v. Hovey, 106-7
Morgan, General John H., 64, 75, 86

Morton, Oliver P., 15, 25, 36, 37, 48, 63, 66, 67, 73, 78, 83, 84, 86, 96, 99 100, 104; letter to Lincoln, 83
Murrill, John A., 38

National Guard of Ohio, 13
Negroes, 12, 16, 17, 41, 51, 52
New England, interpretation of Constitution, 21
New England Confederation, 26
Northwest Ordinance of 1787, 10
Northwestern Confederacy, 38, 54, 78
Northwestern Insurrection, 64

Parliament (Great Britain), 9, 21, 23, 27, 104
Patronage system, 33
Peace Convention, 47
Peace Democrats, 63, 68, 83
Peace Meeting (Hartford), 39
Peace party, 39
Perkins, Samuel E., 77
Personal Memoirs (Grant), 69
Phillips, Wendell, 37
Prize Cases (U.S. Supreme Court), 98

Radical Republicans, 63, 102
Republican party, xi, 3, 6, 15, 16, 17, 18, 26, 27, 33-34, 36, 37, 41, 45, 47, 50, 61, 66, 67, 73, 74, 75, 78, 80, 81, 83, 85, 86, 88, 95, 99, 100, 101, 104, 107, 113, 114
Revolution of 1688-1689 (Great Britain), 21
Roche, John, 88, 89, 106
Roman Catholic Church, 7, 36

Schofield, John M., 62
Secessionists, 64
Second Institute (Coke), 21
Sectionalists, 49
Sedition Act of 1798, 76, 112
Seward, William, 37

Seymour, Horatio, 53
Shay's Rebellion, 38
Sheridan, General Philip Henry, 68
Sherman, General William T., 68, 81, 82
Sixth Amendment, 22
Slack, James R., 16, 17, 24, 65, 66, 104, 106; as colonel of 47th Regiment, 25; meeting with Milligan, 25-26, 49
Slavery, 10, 11, 16, 35, 67; colonial basis of, 12; compared to white servitude, 12; Lincoln's attitude toward, 35
Sons of Liberty, 63, 64, 67, 88, 106, 107
Stamp Act Congress of 1765, 26
Stanton, Edwin M., viii, 59, 99, 100
State sovereignty, 9, 21, 79, 80; change in (1861), 8; Jefferson on, 9
States' rights, 45, 78, 80
Stephens, Alexander H., 10, 11
Stevens, Thaddeus, 102

Taney, Chief Justice Roger B., 95, 97, 98, 100
Tariff controversy, 11, 12
Tenth Amendment, 8, 22
Tories, 21, 39, 66
Trial of the Constitution by Sidney G. Fisher, The, 65

Union Central Committee, 41
Union party, 40, 52, 66, 80
United States Circuit Court, 103, 106
United States Congress, 3, 8, 13, 15, 22, 25, 33, 35, 36, 47, 58, 59, 65, 77, 97, 98, 101-3, 104, 107, 113, 114
United States Constitution, vii, 4, 8, 9, 10, 11, 12, 13, 15, 20, 21, 23, 24, 28, 35, 38, 39, 41, 47, 49, 51, 52, 54, 58, 59, 62, 65, 68, 73, 74,

Index

77, 80, 81, 82, 86, 95, 99, 100, 101, 104; Article IV, 12; Article V, 8, 65; Article VII, 8
United States Supreme Court, viii, 4, 23, 77, 86, 87, 95, 96, 97, 98, 99, 100, 101 102

Vallandigham Clement L., 3, 47, 53, 60, 67, 73, 76, 80, 82, 83, 98, 115; arrested, 73, 76, 83; nomination of, 53; and writ of habeas corpus, 76
Voorhees, Daniel W., 47, 73, 74, 78

Wabash Railroad, viii
War Democrats, 16, 17, 27, 36, 40, 45, 49, 104
War of 1812, 11, 39, 66
Washington, George, 10, 22, 23, 25, 38, 39, 64, 65, 67
Webster, Daniel, 23, 27
Whigs, 16, 21
Winter, Samuel F., 18, 37, 45
Wright, Joseph A., 40

Zumro, H. S., 86